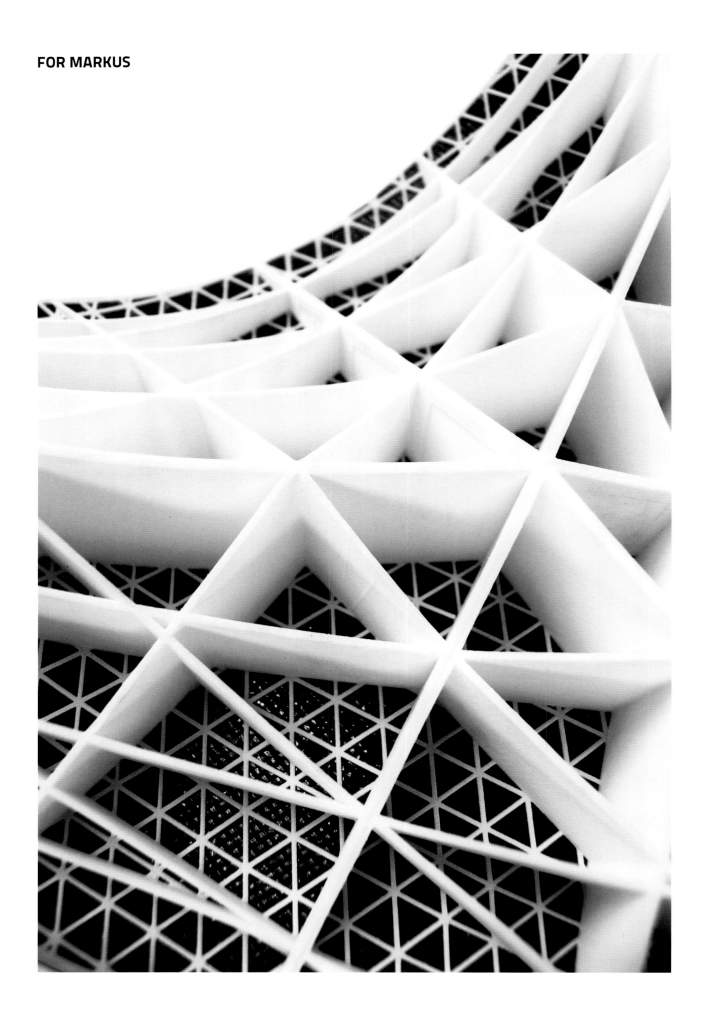

DES IGN FUTU RES

BRADLEY QUINN

MERRELL
LONDON · NEW YORK

INTRODUCTION

The future has been with us from the beginning, ready and waiting to contain all the events yet to happen. Preparing for it occupies the thoughts of most design professionals, who have to interpret the lifestyle shifts unfolding today in order to design the products we will need tomorrow. Designers seem to move between two worlds, creating in the now yet anticipating the future markets in which their products will sell. Short-term strategies can spark long-term trends, and as designers produce new prototypes today and forge fresh directions for tomorrow, they shape the future.

Today's designers and architects are no longer limited by the constraints of the past. For much of modern history, design was regarded as a craft skill, regulated by guild standards established in the Middle Ages. For much of history, fabrication has been limited to a handful of materials, and aesthetics have been slow to change, with high-quality products far beyond most people's reach. In recent years, the industry has undergone radical changes, breaking free of the traditional principles that once constrained it. Contemporary design practice is now permeated with a plethora of new technologies, and increasingly influenced by scientific knowledge. Incorporating nanotechnology, robotics, smart materials and technological interfaces into everyday products may have once seemed like the manifesto of the future, but for many designers it is now standard practice.

Collaborative projects between scientists and designers have opened up exciting new directions for both disciplines. Nanotechnology and robotics are making possible the design of self-assembly structures made from nano-particles that break down and reassemble themselves in new forms. Such designs are being engineered to be self-powering, while other products are driven by new types of energy derived from surprising sources. Replication technology is making it possible to manufacture products at home, revolutionizing the way in which objects are designed, produced and consumed.

Not all of today's groundbreaking designs are rooted in new technology. Dutch designers have found inspiration in simple craft traditions and such concepts as deconstruction, while practitioners working in Japan, the United Kingdom, Denmark and Sweden have created sculptural objects that resemble contemporary art more than industrial design. High-end designs have forged exciting dialogues with contemporary art, striving to speak the same language as they woo a new public ready to embrace edgy products. The spectrum of products known as 'good design' is no longer focused solely on aesthetics and functionality, but created with the tastes, lifestyles and status of its potential buyers in mind. That is not to say that all good design is made to be a luxury object; a wide range of challenging, experimental designs is emerging that criticizes prestige and subverts high-end aesthetics. As in the case of artists who make searing commentaries on cultural politics and social values, designers are also gaining a critical edge, using their work to challenge assumptions and voice dissent.

Yet apart from the innovative visual effects and intellectual narratives, design is also creating a universal language. Products made from environmentally friendly materials and designs created by craft practices are among the icons of the sustainable movement. Designers are making globalism and multiculturalism the norm as they build cultural and economic bridges between East

The purpose of this book is not to attempt to predict the future, but to outline the key factors that have the potential to shape the design and architecture of tomorrow

PAGES 8–9
Sonumbra, a light-emitting parasol designed by London-based research studio Loop.pH, is crafted from a network of electroluminescent fibres. The pattern generated by the parasol responds to ambient sound, glowing and pulsing as noise levels increase. By day, the parasol provides shelter from the sun; by night, it uses the energy collected by the solar cells embedded in its canopy to illuminate its surroundings.

and West, resulting in democratic products that unite societies rather than stratify and divide them. The drive to make good design universally available portends a new economy based on abundance rather than scarcity, leading to future forms rooted in egalitarianism more than elitism.

The purpose of this book is not to attempt to predict the future, but to outline the key factors that have the potential to shape the design and architecture of tomorrow. Leading practitioners within the fields of design and architecture were interviewed for this book, and each chapter features interviewees who explain, in their own words, how they believe their field will develop in the coming years. The book begins by examining the types of cities and buildings being planned for the future, with the opening chapter anticipating how tomorrow's cityscapes will unfold, and the roles that architecture and design will play. Agriculture and architecture will combine in spectacular ways, and the new wave of bio-buildings promises to make them indistinguishable.

The following chapter, 'Interactive Interiors', takes a look inside the dwellings of the future. Homes and offices are being designed to interact with inhabitants, follow their daily routines and anticipate their needs. Flexible architectural components will morph and reconfigure in order to rearrange floor plans, while whole buildings will rotate and revolve to afford residents with a different view or shade them when the sun is at its brightest. Many of these structures will be built from materials featured in the third chapter, which outlines some of the groundbreaking substances that are making our world stronger, smarter, greener, lighter in weight and brighter in appearance.

Future worlds will be constantly evolving, and individual designs will be created with new dynamics that make them multifunctional, interactive and even empathetic. The fourth chapter, 'Dynamic Design', features a selection of designs created with innovations that make life more comfortable and information more accessible. Even sustainable designs will be underpinned with hi-tech dynamics, as scientists and technologists make it possible to reproduce some of nature's own processes in product form. Such innovations, among many others, are radically redefining the role of the surface. The penultimate chapter outlines the innovations that are reinventing it, revealing that few designs created in the future will be described as merely 'surface deep'. They will break down the distinctions between surface and structure, and redraw the boundaries of ordinary, three-dimensional Euclidean space.

The significance of emerging trends is widely recognized within architecture and design, yet few practitioners are able to use this knowledge to their advantage. The final chapter outlines some of the main movements shaping the future directions of these industries, giving practitioners a strategic advantage as they use them to anticipate the trends to come. As designers and architects explore current inspirations and spark new trends, they are playing a key role in creating the future.

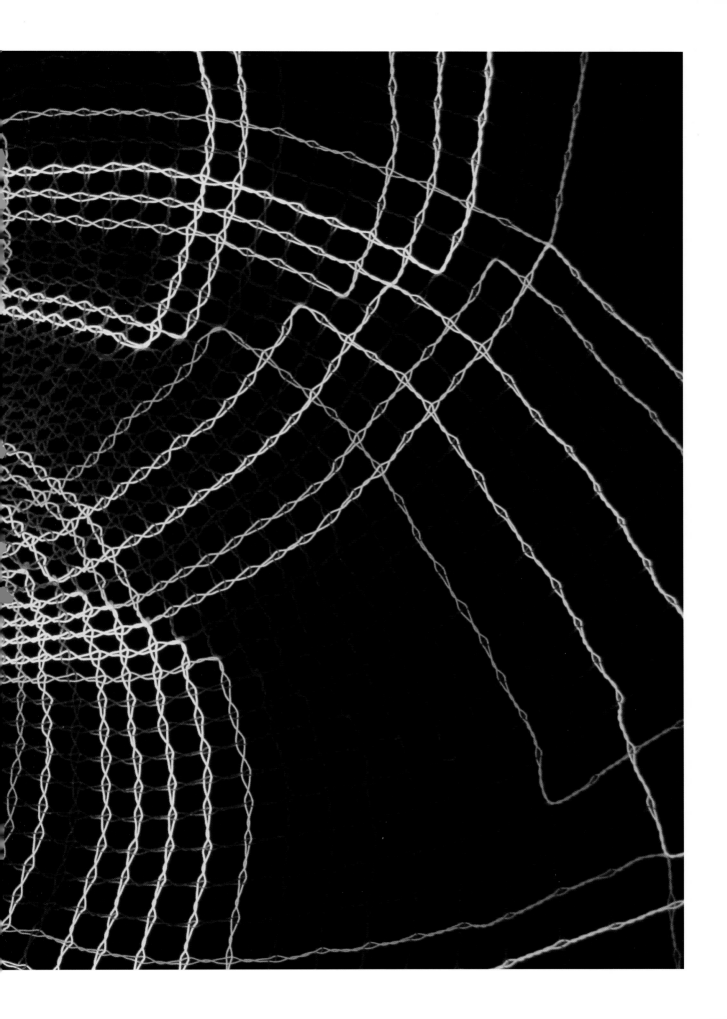

URBAN UTOPIA

BIO-BUILDINGS
BIOSPHERES
URBAN AGRICULTURE

Interviews with
DANIEL LIBESKIND
TOYO ITO

AS

Architecture, design, science and technology are more closely interlinked today than ever before, and the synergy among them is opening up a new world of possibilities

From a present-day perspective, the creation of a future utopia seems inextricably linked to the pursuit of an ideal society. History has revealed the futility of that endeavour, and science fiction provides endless accounts of the dystopias that fallen utopias are likely to create. Yet today's societies are setting out utopian visions for the future, and designers and architects are playing a central role in bringing them to life. The goals of sustainability and zero waste promise to rebalance nature and man, while global communications networks, real-time data transmissions and interactive media hubs are taking us towards a hi-tech future. Architecture, design, science and technology are more closely interlinked today than ever before, and the synergy among them is opening up a new world of possibilities.

One of the most radical changes taking place in urban centres today is the drive to give cities an intelligence of their own. As city centres begin to evolve, they are being reconceived as communications hubs for a wide range of technological exchanges. Just as wireless technologies are now incorporated into existing buildings or seamlessly integrated into new ones, networked intelligence is becoming an integral part of the cityscape, and is being factored into the fabrication of public spaces and municipal facilities. Keeping pace with the ever-accelerating transmission of information is now a central concern for urban planners, and a driving force for the cities of the future. Endowed with artificial intelligence and reconceived as fully automated, self-powering, diagnostic and regenerative, the city will think for itself, and make decisions for its residents too.

Each part of the future city will feature municipal power points and communications hubs, enabling residents to experience many aspects of urban life virtually. Such wearable technological interfaces as visors and wireless headsets will be an integral means of experiencing urban life, downloading and relaying real-time information about the areas through which residents are passing. Those without wireless hardware may rely on synaptic interfaces implanted in the brain to decode optical signals that steer them along predetermined routes or warn of dangers or delays. As urbanites become increasingly reliant on sensor networks to perceive the cityscape and interact with it, few will fully switch off from the world around them. Residents will traverse the city in 'bubbles' of individual technology that can either interlink personal experience with the collective sphere or disconnect from it.

In a responsive, intelligent and fully mobile urban realm, the notion of 'fixed' will disappear altogether. The concept of fluidity will introduce novel ways of both building the city and experiencing it. Along with electronics, future architecture will integrate bio-chemicals into structural parts. Buildings will be designed to transform slowly and change with the seasons, or automatically adjust to shifts in the weather, making inert materials a thing of the past. Fluid forms will not be limited to architecture; parks, parking, roadways and transport hubs will also adjust to compensate for weather conditions. Because the built environment will be constructed from materials that initiate changes from the molecular level, the city itself will be an ever-evolving landscape that reconfigures constantly.

Belgian architects Samyn and Partners designed this as-yet unbuilt structure for the interior of an existing building in Brussels. Featuring built-in photovoltaic panels, the structure is far more sustainable than the building that will house it.

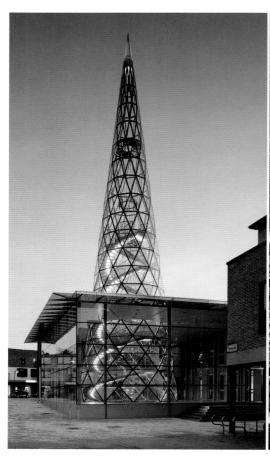

TOP, LEFT AND RIGHT
Samyn and Partners' Centre for
Contemporary Glass Art in Lommel,
Belgium, which opened in 2006.
The spiralling tower complements
the city's existing skyline while
creating a landmark that draws
attention to the futuristic
architecture of the building beneath
it. Although the tower may mimic
a roof, it is actually regarded as
the centre's fifth façade; it was
also designed to form a dramatic
backdrop to the glass art displayed
within the main building. At night,
the tower is illuminated by
electroluminescent diodes that
spiral upwards to form a point
at the top.

BOTTOM
An artist's rendering of the
development planned for the old
Fiera Milano site in the heart of
Milan. The commission to design a
masterplan for the site was won by
Studio Daniel Libeskind, which is
now working in collaboration with
architects Zaha Hadid, Arata Isozaki
and Pier Paolo Maggiora to develop
it. Libeskind intends to fold into
one another the spaces that sustain
leisure, living and commerce,
creating zones in which information
will be accessed wirelessly.

Cities will include buildings that can revolve, similar to the eighty-storey skyscraper designed by Italian architect David Fisher for construction in Dubai. The building will be fitted with micro wind turbines on every level, providing each floor with enough power to rotate around a central structural column. Each floor will be able to turn independently of the others, enabling residents to rotate their quarters according to the view they desire.

Architectural surfaces will take on a new dynamic, adding to the cityscape's ever-shifting persona. Urban façades will become fully integrated with digital media, radically redefining not only their appearance but also their ability to brand themselves. The LED (light-emitting diode) displays developed at the end of the twentieth century will evolve dramatically in the future, with integrated photovoltaic cells harvesting solar energy by day for use after nightfall. GreenPix, the zero-energy media wall developed by Simone Giostra & Partners and Arup, is a visionary example of how multimedia digital systems and photovoltaic technology can be incorporated into a building's façade. Designed for the Xicui entertainment complex in Beijing, the media wall consists of matrices of individual lights embedded in the building's skin. The wall can be used to display animations and create spectacular light effects.

In fact, every aspect of urban architecture will be responsive in future, not only because the façades will illuminate and change shape, but also because the exteriors will be conceived as sensitive skins that harness energy while shielding the structure against wind, rain and solar heat. In addition to drawing light into the building, such exteriors will be endowed with an epidermis-like ability to absorb oxygen and moisture, wicking air and rainwater inside to supply the habitat with necessary resources. Sleek, multidirectional wind turbines will be attached to urban buildings to harness wind energy and provide residents with a sustainable power source.

As new paradigms of the cityscape unfold, traditional architectural boundaries will begin to dissolve. Waterfront areas, in particular, will take on new significance as they are transformed into urban 'hydroscapes'. Climate-change projections indicate that cities in the northern hemisphere are likely to experience more intense rainfall and rising sea levels, meaning that the role of shoreline structures will be reconsidered. As in the case of other parts of the city, they will contain residential and commercial areas, but be built with the barrier-like functions of levees and dykes. Areas vulnerable to being submerged are likely to be replaced by artificial islands that buoy upwards as water levels rise. Such proposals as Lilypad, architect Vincent Callebaut's vision for an amphibious city, provide urban dwellers with a waterborne counterpart to the terrestrial city. Constructed with an outer skin made from polyester fibres coated with titanium dioxide, Lilypad is based on the large floating leaves of the great *Victoria amazonica* water lily. It was conceived as a self-sufficient satellite that will float in close proximity to the shoreline, with its residents growing their own food in vertical gardens and subsurface aquaculture fields. Spring tides and surging currents will become sources of hydroelectric energy, complementing wind turbines and photovoltaic power sources.

Beyond practical needs, today's cityscapes are also built to reflect economic power and social prestige, resembling an architectural stock exchange where social and corporate kudos can boom or crash. In future, corporations will be less inclined to dominate city skylines, and more likely to anchor their offices closer to the ground. Current trends to relocate corporate offices to low, lateral buildings built on semi-rural compounds attest to the growing power of the digital workforce, who often work remotely and have little need of corporate office space. When internet giant Google relocated its corporate headquarters to the cluster of low-rise buildings it calls 'Googleplex', the move revealed how the economic and social benefits of a bucolic base can be enjoyed by corporate bosses and office staff alike. Situated in parkland where staff can walk along trails and have waterfront access, Googleplex has an architectural 'footprint' that is greener than that of an urban tower. As extensions to the urban realm, such corporate campuses will be seen as satellites rather than suburbs, places where the pace of big business is balanced by the harmony of a green lifestyle.

Companies and individuals opting to remain in urban centres may spurn towering skyscrapers in favour of the subterranean structures known as 'subscrapers' or 'groundscrapers'. The concept was pioneered by Malaysian architect Ken Yeang, whose high-rise-like structures are designed to be built inside an excavated area of the bedrock beneath the city. As in the case of troglodyte dwellings that benefit from the temperate conditions found several metres below ground level, the ambient temperature in a subscraper would remain stable irrespective of the changing seasons or shifts in weather. Structures situated beneath the ground are closer to the geothermal power sources created by

the Earth's natural heat, which is regarded as a stable alternative to fluctuating windpower and solar heat. Subscrapers designed with transparent photovoltaic roofs can also harness the sun's energy, channelling light and solar power down to their lower floors. Greenhouse-like areas situated in their upper strata could cultivate vegetation, which would purify the air and boost oxygen levels. Subscrapers, as in the case of buildings with responsive façades and fluid forms, create urban biospheres centred on biodynamics rather than building construction.

These interfaces with the natural world are shaping the architecture to come, making the cities of the future as organic as nature itself. The three sections that follow describe the emerging developments that will bring urban environments and nature closer together in the future. The first section, 'Bio-buildings', charts the impact of biomimetics on architecture and living spaces, while 'Biospheres', the section following it, describes the possibility of sealing future communities within biodynamic enclosures. The last section, 'Urban Agriculture', looks at how crop cultivation and building construction are beginning to merge, resulting in cityscapes that resemble farms, and architecture that appears to be edible. The chapter concludes with interviews with Daniel Libeskind and Toyo Ito, who share their visions of how future architecture will be conceived.

The creation of Dutch architect Winka Dubbeldam, these pavilions have been designed for a new 'green' zone in Brussels. Each pavilion is enveloped by a structural skin, a continuous concrete membrane, into which skylights, solar collectors and ducts for gathering rainwater have been integrated. The buildings will generate their own energy supplies and channel rainwater throughout the green zone, including to a series of greenhouses. In summer, the green zone will be cooled by fountains that diffuse water in the form of a mist.

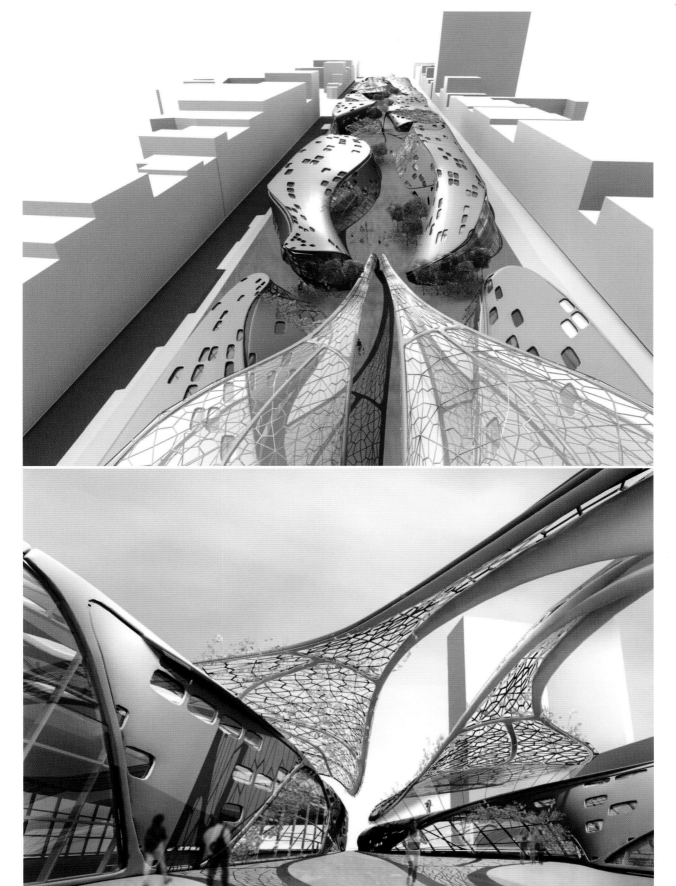

BIO-BUILDINGS

A sustainable cityscape calls for green materials and environmentally friendly construction methods, and recent scientific research suggests a promising future for both. Thanks to the science of biomimicry, which studies the models, systems and processes of animals and plants, nature's know-how can be harnessed to create new horizons for architectural design. Biomimetic architecture takes nature's lead, and fuses high-tech designs with basic cellular functions. The resultant buildings perform in the same way as living organisms, redrawing the boundaries between nature and architecture.

Although the science of biomimicry is new, the principles behind it are not. Mankind has long used technology to imitate nature. Leonardo da Vinci's flying machine mimicked outspread wings, and commercial airliners take their ergonomic shape from birds' bodies and beaks. The telephone receiver is modelled on the anatomy of the human ear, and animal dwellings and plants have inspired architectural shapes and surfaces for many centuries. Translated architecturally, biomimetic principles can create environments and whole buildings that operate like natural organisms, sensing and reacting to climatic changes as well as the needs of their inhabitants. This nature-inspired approach to the cityscape is based on a biomimetic model of an ever-evolving ecosystem. Rather than being built from unyielding materials forever fixed to the bedrock beneath them, cities will be both anchored to specific points and able to 'move' within a set of predetermined parameters.

The project known as Habitat 2020, a revolutionary form of housing planned for construction in rural China, exemplifies the application of biomimetic technology. Philips Electronics has designed the housing, a series of eco-friendly tower blocks, as an example of a sustainable urban community powered by 'off the grid' energy sources. Each building features an organic membrane, which creates a living link between the structure's inert materials and the landscape around it. Intended to mimic the stomata of a leaf, pore-like openings in the membrane re-create the transpiration of plants. The membrane can absorb moisture from the air, and channels sunlight, air and rainwater into the building, which automatically rotates to face the sun as it moves through the sky. Air and rainwater are filtered naturally as they are drawn into the building, and any biogases not converted to energy can be vented through the membrane. Because Habitat 2020 mimics a plant-based ecosystem more than an urban community, its environmental footprint is dramatically lower than that of conventional buildings.

From his practice in Charlottesville, Virginia, award-winning architect William McDonough has applied biomimetic thinking to his futuristic Treescraper Tower of Tomorrow. As the name suggests, McDonough's tower is a high-rise designed to mimic the form and functions of a tree. The building's curvilinear shape gives it an aerodynamic profile similar to that of a tree trunk. The water used in the building is drawn upwards from groundwater and circulated by means that are similar to a tree's own circulatory systems. Waste water is recycled in the tower's garden, and run-off water from the planting beds is re-used in a grey-water facility. Harnessing the power of the sun, solar panels are positioned strategically on the exterior in a manner that mimics the arrangement

TOP
Growing and evolving in the manner of a living being, this organic building in Linkebeek, Belgium, seems more vegetable than architectural. Designed by Samyn and Partners, the structure is insulated by the vegetation clinging to three of its four walls. Discrete irrigation ducts water the plants from within the walls, ensuring that they receive moisture whatever the weather.

BOTTOM
Designed by R&Sie(n), the Paris-based practice of François Roche and Stéphanie Lavaux, this futuristic museum for a site in Switzerland contrasts organic areas with sleek glass walls. The organic façades will contain a selection of exotic plants chosen by a botanical artist; planting will even extend to the roof. The plants' containers, irrigation tubes and fertilization systems will be streamed through a fabric support system anchored to rigid PVC panels.

The front façade of Samyn and Partners' building in Linkebeek (see page 19) shows how the organic exteriors shield it from neighbouring buildings on either side. The façade is constructed from glass panels that capture solar energy and flood the building with natural light. In summer, netting is drawn over the glass to create a heat-deflecting screen.

Although these capsule-like Lifepods are easily integrated into nature, Korean-American architect Kyu Che actually designed them with the future urbanite in mind. Made from prefabricated components, Lifepods can be adapted for use in a wide variety of terrains. Lightweight and sustainable, they provide everyone with an easy and ecological means of changing habitats.

of tree branches, which grow in clusters to optimize the exposure of the leaves to sunlight.

Most societies regard insects as inimical to the built environment, and many of today's discussions about sustainable architecture approach the issue from a biomimetic stance. The project known as Mosquito Bottleneck House, created by Paris-based designer Mathieu Lehanneur in collaboration with architect R&Sie(n), defers to the local insect population in remarkable ways. The house was commissioned for a site in Trinidad known for being infested with mosquitoes at certain times of the year. To overcome the problem, Lehanneur designed the house as a dual habitat: one for humans to live in, and one for mosquitoes to travel through on their normal flight path without coming into contact with the occupants. Lehanneur created ducts that pass from one side of the house to the other, and lined them with materials that attract mosquitoes. As the insects approach the house, the scent emitted by the material draws them towards the ducts that transverse the building, and therefore away from the areas used by the occupants.

The capsule-like habitats known as Lifepods are lightweight, individual dwellings designed with the future nomad in mind. Intended to hover in the air, float on water and move easily over land, Lifepods will be manufactured using the latest automotive, aeronautic and nautical technologies. They are the creation of San Francisco-based Korean-American architect Kyu Che, whose vision for the dwellings includes prototypes made from prefabricated modular components. Che's Lifepods have footings that easily adjust to the landscape, eliminating the need to reshape the terrain to

create a level base. They can be 'parked' on city streets or perched on rooftops, generate their own power, and filter water and waste. They can also manoeuvre through tranquil water much as barges do, and be suspended above ground by tethers attached to tree trunks or cliff faces. Che's designs are inspired by the transient patterns of roaming animals and migratory birds, and Lifepods give humans an easy and ecological means of changing habitats within the city and beyond it.

BIOSPHERES

Urban societies tend to regard such environmental factors as dust, mould and spores as hostile not only to human health but also to the built environment. Much of the discussion within sustainable architecture revolves around efforts to filter out these threats, or eliminate them altogether. Although the campaign against such biohazards has gained momentum in modern times, the drive to eradicate them is nothing new. Architecture's origins seem rooted in humankind's campaign to expel airborne contaminants, and the war against them is likely to continue long into the future.

Modern cities are host to a wide range of microorganisms, which urban planners attempt to control by restricting access to the environments known to harbour the most harmful. Waste-treatment facilities are usually located well outside city centres, and medical laboratories are subject to strict controls to prevent contaminants from entering the rest of the city. Grey-water schemes, new filtration technology and compost-sanitation systems will eventually make waste-treatment plants redundant, and rapid advancements in biocontainment systems are minimizing the risk of contaminants leaching into the environment. Future cities will also take preventative measures to detect and eradicate airborne pathogens that lead to disease, and neutralize any organisms considered to be potential agents for bioterrorism.

Large-scale artificial biomes, such as the Eden Project in Cornwall, England, and the Montreal Biodome (a structure distinct from the Montreal Biosphère shown opposite), reveal the extent to which architecture can be used to create climatically and geographically defined ecosystems both within urban areas and outside them. Biosphere 2, for example, a sealed ecosystem in Arizona built by John Ophus, re-creates natural ecologies and human habitations in order to observe the synergy between man, agriculture and technology. When the biosphere's structure is sealed, scientists are able to monitor and control changes in the air, water and soil to optimize their effects. The biosphere's technical systems present a model for future urban infrastructures. Independent piping systems circulate heat and cooling water, and recycling systems support the zero-waste policy. Solar energy is harnessed from the glass panels covering most of the surface area, and natural gases are harvested on site to provide further power sources.

Although the research collected by the scientists managing Biosphere 2 was initially intended to facilitate the eventual construction of sealed biospheres in space, the resulting data may also be applied to the creation of biospheres on Earth. Built structures capable of managing the microclimate of an entire city can engineer their ecosystems to operate independently of the macro-environments surrounding them. According to the Gaia hypothesis, which states that the Earth is a complex, self-regulating system of physical and chemical interactions, such biospheres can be regarded as living organisms, making them consistent with models of architecture that re-interpret the cityscape as an organic, reactive entity. In an urban biosphere, biotic and abiotic factors could be specifically engineered to create optimal ecosystems, enabling communities and their architectural environments to work together as a single system.

TOP
Geodesic domes have been in existence for nearly one hundred years, and have always presented a model for futuristic structures. Many modern versions are based on the omnitriangulated shape of fullerene molecules, making them extremely strong yet relatively lightweight. The Montreal Biosphère, shown here, is a museum dedicated to researching water conservation, sustainable development and new ecosystems.

BOTTOM
By re-creating natural ecologies so that they can be studied, the Montreal Biosphère highlights the role of architecture in creating climatically and geographically defined ecosystems. The building's technical systems present a model for future urban infrastructures.

URBAN AGRICULTURE

Food, like architecture, has always played a key role in shaping urban life. Local farming has been a crucial determinant of a city's food culture, and has contributed to its economy on many levels. Historically, the boundaries between urban living and agricultural production have been distinct; in the future, the two will come closer together, perhaps even merging into a single system of food cultivation.

Biomimetic architecture and biosphere environments promise to reinvent the urban landscape as a biodynamic system that will contribute to the city's food production and supply. No longer performed elsewhere, the cultivation of food will become an essential part of public space and an everyday aspect of city life. Urban agriculture will become part of the city's infrastructure, overlapping with such areas of the public sector as health, education and planning. This trend can already be seen on city rooftops, where previously unused spaces have been converted into kitchen gardens. Similarly, restaurants are increasingly growing many of their own ingredients: some rent allotments near city centres, while others grow fruit and vegetables on rooftops, in courtyards and in converted car parks.

Instead of using roofs made from traditional materials, architects are beginning to top their structures with tracts of fertile turf, providing residential and commercial buildings with arable areas. 'Green' walls, which are also known as 'grow' walls, are covered in vegetation, creating a lush living envelope that provides natural insulation and improves air quality. In many cities, such walls are regarded as vertical gardens on which food can be grown. Turf Design Studio in Sydney has created the Salad Bar, an upright growing frame designed to make the garden more compatible with the verticality of the cityscape. The modular structure angles and elevates the surface area of an average vegetable patch to reduce its footprint on the ground. The designers claim that growing plants vertically maximizes their exposure to light and minimizes their exposure to pests. This enables plants grown on a wall of, say, 3 square metres (32 square feet) to yield more than plants grown in a vegetable patch of a similar size.

Vertical agriculture relies on fertile surfaces, and aeroponic farming is considered to be the most environmentally friendly method of transforming city walls into arable fields. Aeroponics is the process of cultivating plants without the use of soil, which makes the system compatible with most vertical surfaces. In aeroponic farming, plants are grown in air or mist fertilized with liquid nutrients. Although aeroponic farming uses water to transmit nutrients to the plants, the system differs from hydroponics, which uses water as a growing medium. Aeroponics uses one-tenth of the water normally used in soil cultivation, dramatically reducing the water and energy input per square metre (11 square feet) of growing area.

Networks of urban agriculture will link local sites with whole landscapes, and fuse local economies with new ecologies. Architecture's new role within food production will align it with science and agriculture, pushing the frontiers of architecture ever forward. As future architecture manages resources, yields crops and engineers ecosystems, it promises to emerge as a means of embracing the natural environment – even as that environment constantly changes around us.

In an architectural project that pioneered new methods of urban food production, R&Sie(n) cultivated hydroponically sustained ferns. Grown in nutrient beds, the plants were nourished by proteins, bacteria and rainwater. The glass beakers shown here, hand-blown by Italian craftsmen especially for the project, were designed to deliver nutrients to the plants drop by drop.

LEFT
Architecture's emerging role within food production is bringing the frontiers of agriculture ever closer to the heart of the city. Simply called Salad Bar, the growing wall shown here is a vertical garden created by Turf Design Studio in Sydney.

OPPOSITE
As 'green' city projects sweep through urban centres around the world, Turf Design Studio is showing Australians how salads, vegetables and herbs can be cultivated in public spaces across the nation. Measuring approximately 2.5 metres (8 feet) high, the Salad Bars are divided into a series of 1 × 1-metre (3 × 3-feet) modules. Each module is filled with earth and compost, with seedlings planted directly into the soil. Once the various food items are fully grown, city dwellers are invited to pick and eat them.

DANIEL LIBESKIND

Daniel Libeskind is based in New York, but his work transcends virtually all borders. A visionary who explores the boundaries of construction and the possibilities of space, Libeskind creates new environments that map changes in society and new directions for industry. Although he is well known for his built structures, he has spent most of his working life as an architectural theorist, writer and professor. Libeskind did not complete his first built design until he was fifty-two years old, in the late 1990s. His characteristic style was formed in the 1960s, which suggests that his approach evolved several decades before the architectural community was ready for it. In the following interview, Libeskind shares his views on how architecture can be a catalyst for generating new lifestyles and enhancing the quality of urban life.

How will the city of the future take shape?

The future city should blur the lines between commerce and culture, popular and elite, high and low. As much as cultural institutions need to be profitable in order to flourish, so do commercial enterprises need to have a cultural conscience in order to succeed. This intertwining of public and private needs a positive articulation in the city structure. Planning, zoning, land use, transportation – all these have to be radically rethought and redefined in order to bring a true renaissance to city living. The city of the future should no longer be defined by its two-dimensional 'grids' or flattened perspectives, but rather by spatial peaks and valleys, multidimensional parks and water, echoing the landscape that gave it its birth.

Will city residents play a key role?

Future cities need to develop full democratic participation in order to create the kind of public space and living realm that allows everyone to pursue their own dreams. This is not a utopian ideal, even at the scale of the modern city. The empowerment of citizens to participate directly in the design of their own environment is the *conditio sine qua non* of a meaningful future.

Your Futuropolis city concept outlines a new paradigm for urban space. What are the key elements?

Futuropolis is about space. It is not about fashion. It is not about decoration. It is about creating something that cannot be repeated.

It is about, for example, carving out a space for trees. It is carving out a space where nature can enter the domestic world of a city. A space where something that has never seen the light of day can enter into the inner workings of a dense structure. That is really the nature of architecture. Cities are mirrors of the complex historical realities that went into their making. However, precisely because cities are both producers and consumers of new ideas, they shatter tradition and continuity through their own progress. The issue is not how high the buildings are, but the height of human aspiration. Futuropolis represents a new theatre of memory, bridging the conceptual and the material, the individual and the collective, identity and difference. Light, space, proportion, materials, music and stories give every person the freedom to participate in the creative process.

Can future cities be built upon existing ones?

The twenty-first century will be the century of cities; the city of the future is no longer a fantasy but a reality. As cities become more dense, and as the complexity of modern life transforms their very structure, the exploration of the future is no longer a luxury but a necessity. The transformation of contemporary cities can take an unfortunate dystopian turn: the shrinking of public spaces, the lack of nature and fresh air, the challenges of transportation and the separation of economic classes. Conversely, a positive evolution of the city can lead to a greater awareness of how to use limited resources in order to create democratic,

diverse, beautiful and sustainable cities. Design and architecture should respond to all this in a spiritual and philosophical sense. It's not simply a matter of more of the same; rather, it's the desire once again to base architecture on human beings – on children, on families – not just on computer manipulation and abstraction. We must do this in order to put forth truly creative, radical and controversial ideas, and advance architecture into the future.

What will characterize future cities?

They will be based on such factors as empowering citizens to be involved in the creative process of change in a meaningfully collaborative way, not just giving a 'yes' or 'no' at a community meeting; private–public partnerships that create bold scenarios by dispensing with old ideologies; and regarding the city as the greatest repository of human dreams and desires – a dynamic work of art whose creators, mostly anonymous, link up across the generations.

What will be the city's central focus in future?

The test of the future city will be how a child's well-being and imagination are fired into the future. In the fiction of monetary utopias, the city is no longer humanity written large, and humankind is a city written very small and almost illegibly. This has to be reversed, so that once again humanity is written large, and is at the centre of a great city.

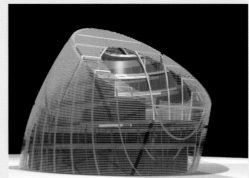

TOP LEFT
Libeskind has been commissioned to design the masterplan for the new Yongsan business district in Seoul. Conceived as an extensive urban park, the site will feature clusters of residential, office and retail neighbourhoods on the banks of the Han River. Libeskind says that he intends to 'make each form, each place and each neighbourhood as varied and distinctive as possible. The plan, and each building within it, should reflect the vertical and cultural complexity of the heart of Seoul.'

CLOCKWISE FROM TOP RIGHT
In the northern Italian city of Brescia, Libeskind is designing eight residential buildings as part of the redevelopment of the Sannazzaro neighbourhood. Libeskind's scheme spirals outwards from a sphere-like core structure, creating a new hub for the city. His plans also introduce sustainability, public space, commerce and leisure into an existing urban landscape.

TOYO ITO

Tokyo-based Toyo Ito is one of the world's most innovative and influential architects. Although Ito's designs are conceptual in origin, he is a master of built structures. Many of his designs are characterized by sculptural, sensual contours of poured concrete, with textured exteriors giving way to smooth glass surfaces. Others are based on fluid spaces, seamless structures and cloudy translucence, ideas that seem to dematerialize architecture rather than validate it. Ito was an early pioneer of technological interfaces and interactive surfaces, but has since promoted a new approach to architecture based on creating individual structures and whole cities that mimic natural forms. Below, Ito considers how architecture might evolve, and explains how technology and the natural world can coexist in the future.

What is your vision for the architecture of the future?

The architecture of the future should merge with the natural environment and adapt to changes just as nature does. This idea is the opposite of the machine analogy of architecture that emerged during the twentieth century, which led architects to focus on functionalistic systems rather than think in terms of the natural environment. As a result, today's architecture doesn't often relate to its surroundings, but future architecture has to, and it should be conceived as a life form rather than merely as a built structure. I see futuristic architecture as a living, breathing life form integrated with the natural environment.

How can a new paradigm of naturalistic architecture be achieved?

To make that happen, a dramatic transformation needs to occur, which revolutionizes the concept of architecture itself. Merging architecture with the natural environment will require an integrated planning and engineering design methodology, but will also need a radical reformation within government administrations and the social systems that are related to architectural education, construction and design.

How will design contribute to the development of naturalistic architecture?

The design of form is not an issue, but the actual function of architecture is. So, rather than merely finding technical solutions to ecological and sustainability problems of the twenty-first century, architects should instead try to use their design skills to change people's awareness and expectations of architecture.

Is it possible to create 'living, breathing' architecture through technological means?

Advances in computer technology blur the borders of design, construction and the actual use of architecture. From the early stages of design, people can already begin to experience architecture virtually through the computer screen, and of course living, breathing architectural designs can also be developed through such simulation. But when it comes to more intricately designed projects, mock-ups and maquettes would be necessary to facilitate such an integrated process.

Which materials are shaping future architecture?

Steel and concrete will remain as the main structural materials for the time being. An appreciation of wooden construction has recently re-emerged, and will be widely applied to large-scale buildings. I don't expect any structural or finishing materials to emerge in the near future that will exceed the ones used widely today.

Ito's design for the Taichung Metropolitan Opera House in Taiwan signals a move away from conventional rectilinear architecture. The design is an open structure intended to break down boundaries between the performing arts. By limiting the number of enclosed spaces in the building, Ito hopes to foster new relationships between high art and popular culture, visitors and performers, stage and auditorium, and interior and exterior. Ito regards the opera house as a flexible acoustic space equipped with a series of 'sound caves' for performances and rehearsals, as well as areas designated for use as foyers, restaurants and offices.

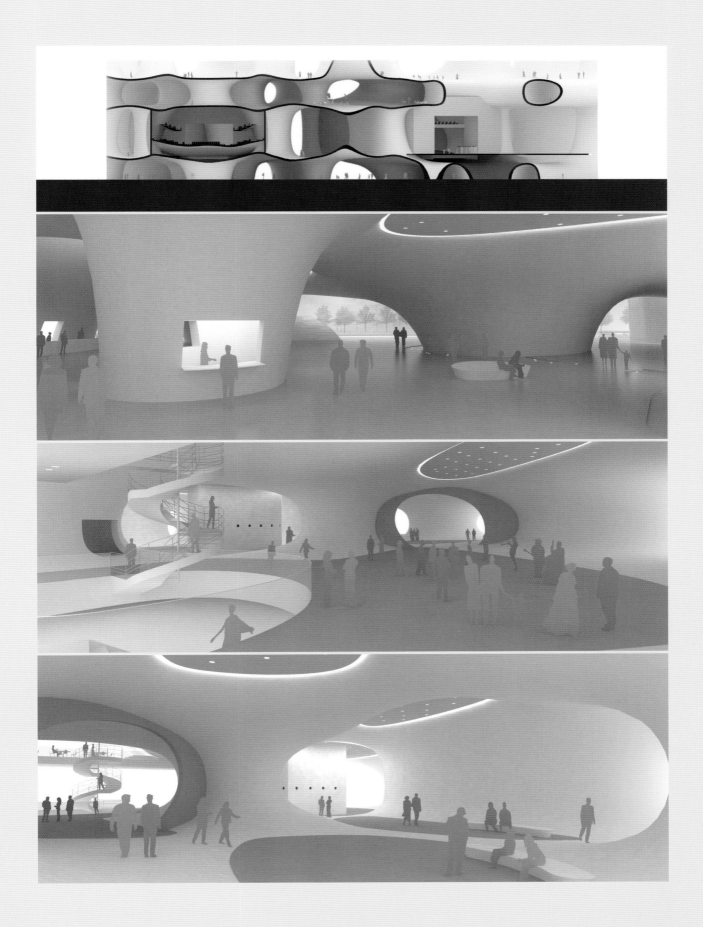

INTERA
INTERI

SOFT ARCHITECTURE
SOOTHING SPACES
REVOLUTIONARY ROOMS
RESIDENT ROBOTS

Interviews with
WINKA DUBBELDAM
KARIM RASHID

ACTIVE
ORS

Future interiors, like the buildings that will house them, will be intelligent and responsive, adjusting to short-term changes or reconfiguring to meet new parameters

At a time when technology, flexibility and multifunctionality are key considerations for urban architecture, interiors are also being equipped with interactive potential. Future interiors, like the buildings that will house them, will be intelligent and responsive, adjusting to short-term changes or reconfiguring to meet new parameters. As a tool for urban life, the interior will be flexible enough to accommodate the needs of the future human, and will easily adapt to suit their lifestyle. Shifts in the residents' routines will be detected by diagnostic technology programmed to monitor their daily movements and relay them to automated systems integrated within the interior's infrastructure. Designed to be self-regulating, the interior will think for itself, compensate for shortcomings and constantly monitor its residents in order to maximize their levels of comfort.

The home of the future will emerge as a hybrid space that fuses lifestyle choices and leisure interests with the professional obligations of the occupants. Embedded technology and invisible computerized systems will become an everyday aspect of domestic life. Online information forums and virtual-reality platforms will be an integral part of the interior, and will no longer be seen as something separate from the physical world. Together with interactive technology, virtual-reality software will transform the home environment into a responsive and even empathetic sensory space. The interior's ability to discern the moods of individuals will enable the home actively to soothe or energize the inhabitants. The overriding presence of technology will not seem intrusive to homeowners, but will evolve as a tool that amplifies the synergy between people and their homes.

As technology equips surfaces and appliances with interfaces able to monitor the environments around them, they will also become capable of interacting with systems outside the home. Feedback loops will be embedded in household items and interior accessories to monitor our relationships with the objects we live with. The data they transmit will provide manufacturers with information that will enable them to improve the performance of their products, even in real time. The new technology will encourage the interior to form networks with organizations outside the home, and even to establish relationships with similar environments in order to share knowledge and conserve resources. The interior will join networks that better facilitate the domestic needs of the residents and participate on platforms that strengthen their social sphere. While the home will still be a refuge, it will no longer be a place where the occupants can hide.

Today, most people would argue that their lifestyle shapes the environment in which they live, but in the future, individuals will tend to use their living space to determine the type of life they lead. With the integration of communications platforms, the stream of information that flows into the home will shape the occupants' movements both within it and outside it. So-called 'nudge' technology will give residents 'prompts' throughout the day to help them maintain personal goals, meet deadlines and focus their attention constructively. The efficiency of a technologized home will be seen as conducive to creating an unwavering, methodical mindset that eliminates the sort of anxiety associated with living in chaos and clutter. Working from home will be the norm for many professionals, whose absence from

The Switch bar and restaurant in Dubai features a continuous, contouring wall that collapses the distinctions between floor and ceiling. Designed by Karim Rashid, the space is also characterized by dramatic interplays between light and shadow inspired by the sand dunes in the desert outside the city. The artwork on the ceiling is backlit to reveal a series of inspirational phrases in Arabic script.

OPPOSITE
The interior of the Switch bar and restaurant (see page 37) features many of the elements that help to define Karim Rashid's distinctive style. His use of pastel colours, bold geometric patterns and curvilinear shapes signals a shift away from the cool minimalism of the 1990s and 2000s, presenting a palette of bright colours and soft shapes for the future.

PAGES 40–41
Spanish designer Jaime Hayón teamed up with Italian energy company Enel to consider the role of energy in future interiors. The resulting installation consists of a grid-like black-and-white structure fitted with low-energy LED lights throughout and a collection of sustainable energy sources. Inside the structure, Hayón installed a tabletop covered in photovoltaic cells, a cabinet equipped with small wind turbines and several self-propelled, rotating ceramic forms.

the workplace will be filled by a holograph. An extension of an interactive database, the holograph will be able to download data and interact with customers and colleagues. Monitors, screens, keyboards and computer interfaces will have been seamlessly integrated into most household surfaces, enabling residents to carry out their professional duties as they move around the home. The differences between home and office will slowly dissolve: as domestic spaces gain the efficiency of office environments, commercial venues will acquire the comforts of a home.

These new concepts of space will promote a fluid dialogue between architecture, lighting, interior design and inhabitants' needs. Flexible floor plans, moveable walls and adjustable ceilings will be made possible by a new generation of labile materials. The structures that demarcate space will be made from elastic metals, 'memory' materials, ductile plastics and inflatable membranes, making it possible to reposition doorways, corridors, staircases and whole rooms. Interiors designed with this degree of fluidity will require water mains, waste pipes, energy channels and ventilation ducts that are equally elastic. These amenities will contain conduits that can deliver manufacturing materials to the home, creating a flow of the photopolymers and low-viscose silicone-like materials that will enable rapid-manufacturing machines to produce products at home. Rapid-manufacturing technology is predicted to revolutionize the way in which we acquire goods, and will ultimately make it possible for the future interior to manufacture itself.

Some of the key technological developments shaping the interiors of the future are outlined in the following four sections. 'Soft Architecture'

describes how the integration of robotics, materials and interior design will create uniquely flexible living environments, while 'Soothing Spaces' reveals that the recent emphasis on well-being will result in homes with spa-like comforts. 'Revolutionary Rooms' examines interiors made up of shifting spaces, and buildings that rotate and revolve. 'Resident Robots', the final section, explores the extent to which artificial intelligence and automated systems will come to shape our homes and the lives we lead. In feature interviews at the end of the chapter, Winka Dubbeldam and Karim Rashid share their thoughts on the living spaces of the future.

SOFT ARCHITECTURE

An ever-changing interior requires systems of flexible components that can morph into new shapes quickly and easily, and still be able to return to their original form and begin anew. This kind of interior will be built with pliable materials, and constructed within technical and architectural parameters that make it compatible with the systems that enable the building itself to change shape.

A shape-changing wall developed by Mette Ramsgard Thomsen and Karin Bech at the Centre for Information Technology and Architecture in Copenhagen is intended to make interiors interactive. Called Slow Furl, the system of fluid wall components brings robotic technologies and flexible materials together in a structure able to interact with the individuals around it. Still at the prototype stage, Slow Furl consists of a mechanized wooden skeleton covered with a custom-made textile 'skin' woven with conductive copper fibres. When two parts of the textile touch, the conductive fibres trigger the mechanical system to reconfigure the structure into a new shape. As people lean against the structure's surface, or stroke, sit or lie on it, it reacts to their movements and causes the mechanized structure to reform. As it does so, recesses and cavities open up to cradle the human form more comfortably.

The Slow Furl project is pioneering a new approach to interior architecture. Ramsgard Thomsen and Bech's starting point was a mandate to reinterpret the interior in terms of 'flow' and 'responsive surfaces'. 'The embedding of responsive systems influences how we imagine the future experience of architecture', explains Ramsgard Thomsen in an interview with the author. 'In classical and modernist architecture alike, the building is conceived as a structure created to be independent of the human body. Slow Furl achieves the opposite by engaging the inhabitant and guiding them through sequences of changing space. We use digital technologies to dispel the

sense of isolation associated with architecture, allowing the building itself to be interfaced with by the inhabitant.'

Graft, a Los Angeles-based architectural practice, shares the vision for soft architecture, although its approach is to sculpt interiors from rigid materials. Its Hotel Q! in Berlin features an 'interior landscape' made up of a variety of hybrid forms. Sloping surfaces divide the spaces and demarcate areas as a wall would, yet give way to recesses and horizontal surfaces that suggest seating and tabletops. Floors rise to create split-level areas, generating forms that facilitate seating and sleeping. Graft's topologically inspired approach promotes a unique kind of interactivity, since it erases the traditional boundaries between furniture and interior architecture. The firm's 'softened' versions of fixed forms enable individuals to interact with them in multiple ways, depending on how they wish to use them. Walls may form boundaries, yet also facilitate access to other areas as hotel guests walk across them to reach upper levels. Recesses in the floor can provide sunken seating, but can be filled with water and used as a hot tub. As the interior landscape creates a continuous flow of form and space, the fluid shapes folded within its 'terrain' create a seemingly endless spectrum of possible uses.

TOP
The responsive interior-textile system known as Slow Furl encourages individuals to interact with their surroundings. The system provides a tactile interface that promotes a new way of experiencing interior architecture.

BOTTOM
Sensory and robotic, the Slow Furl membranes are programmed to move, flex and reconfigure as they are touched. When a person makes contact with a membrane, embedded conductive fibres trigger the mechanical system to change the membrane's shape.

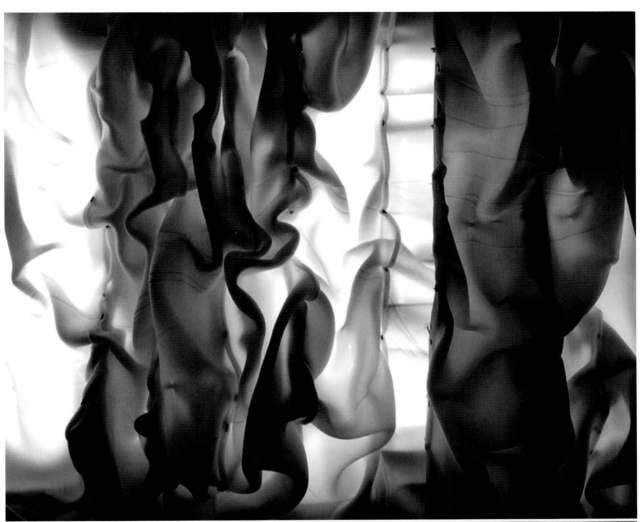

LEFT, TOP
Whether built in Japan or
elsewhere, Japanese tea houses
are always serene structures.
This contemporary tea house was
designed by Japanese architect
Kengo Kuma for the garden of the
Museum für Angewandte Kunst in
Frankfurt. Situated in a tranquil
part of the garden, the tea house
was constructed from inflatable
materials, making it uniquely tactile
and soft.

LEFT, CENTRE AND BOTTOM
Kuma's tea house is not 'built'
like a conventional building,
but designed to take shape as it
inflates. The structure is fabricated
from waterproof textiles divided
into a series of cells that can be
filled with air. LED lighting systems
are integrated into the textiles,
illuminating the preparation room
and dining area.

OPPOSITE, TOP
Designed by Graft, Hotel Q! in
Berlin is architecturally unique.
The interiors are laid out in a
landscape of sloping gradients and
unexpected contours that challenge
conventional perceptions of indoor
space. The floor and wall surfaces
shown here fold inwards to create
alcoves, and buckle upwards to
form seating.

OPPOSITE, BOTTOM
Graft's topographical treatment
of Hotel Q! is also intended to save
space. Here, the distance between
bedroom and bathroom has been
shrunk to almost nothing, with the
bed and bath sitting side by side in
a single unit.

OPPOSITE
The Smart-o-logic concept created
by Karim Rashid explores the
potential for manufacturing modular
dwellings inexpensively and
efficiently. Designed by Rashid for
the Corian Living exhibition in
2010, the concept is a case study
in how technology, furniture and
living areas can work together to
reduce the environmental footprint
of urban spaces.

RIGHT
With its state-of-the-art lighting,
broad surfaces, wall nooks and
alcoves, the Smart-o-logic space
could also provide a blueprint for
future offices and retail boutiques.

SOOTHING SPACES

Well-being has emerged as an important focus for many twenty-first-century men and women, and some of the benefits of holistic treatments will be integrated into the interiors of the future. Architects will equip interiors with technologies that promote relaxation, and commercial environments will be designed to make individuals feel at ease. This holistic approach to interior design is nothing new: the use of architectural space to create sensory experiences is widespread among health facilities, spas and hotels. Many are decorated with designs and colour schemes intended to soothe and calm, or uplift and excite. The feel-good factor generated by such places will become the norm for commercial and domestic spaces of the future.

Just as a therapist dims the lights, scents the room and plays soothing music, sensory technology embedded in the home will adjust environmental factors to simulate a domestic sanctuary. Holographic imagery will be projected to transform the home into a virtual spa, or any type of environment conducive to relaxation. Sound, scent and lighting will be aligned to create a powerful, mood-altering trinity. The synergy between them will be calibrated by mnemonic software and neurological stimulators in order to boost the residents' dopamine levels and promote a steady release of endorphins, thus creating a sense of well-being.

Jenny Tillotson, a researcher based at Central Saint Martins College of Art and Design in London, is exploring the mood-altering applications of sensory and aroma technology. Tillotson is developing a system of sensory interior surfaces that wirelessly monitor the resident's mental state and trigger changes to enhance his or her mood. Known as Scentsory Design, the system comprises a wearable sensor and a series of scent-infused surfaces called Wellpaper. The sensor is programmed with diagnostic technology developed by medical researchers to detect alterations in breathing and skin temperature. Sudden flashes of temperature and changes in breathing are usually indicative of the wearer's mental state, giving the Wellpaper information about the wearer's mood in real time. As in the case of wallpaper, Wellpaper is attached to walls, but is capable not only of emitting a range of scents but also of displaying a wide spectrum of colours. It is powered by electronic circuitry, which pulses the therapeutic scents through a fluidic cabling system embedded in the surface of the material. The release of scent and change of colourways are wirelessly activated by the data signals transmitted by the sensor when it is worn.

Along with colour and scent, lighting plays an important role in creating a soothing atmosphere. The intensity of light and the range of colours it projects can be therapeutic, and are known to produce physical and psychological effects. Lighting can cause headaches or alleviate them, and has been known to lower blood pressure when toned down to soothing levels. Future applications for therapeutic lighting include interior lights that follow the cycle of the human circadian system, which relates changes in the body's biochemical processes to the light–dark patterns created by the Earth's twenty-four-hour orbit. Lighting systems designed to counteract winter-time light deprivation are already in use. Seasonal Affective Disorder (SAD), for example, can be alleviated by lighting that simulates spring/summer daylight levels at darker times of the year. Future applications will not suffuse the interior with a constant blast of daylight

TOP
Researcher Jenny Tillotson creates wearable devices that detect changes in the wearer's emotional state and relay them to his or her clothing and surrounding surfaces. Here, Tillotson has created a whimsical vision of how her Smart Second Skin Dress detects the relaxing effect that music has on the wearer and relays this change in emotions to the surfaces surrounding her.

BOTTOM, LEFT AND RIGHT
A micro-cabling system embedded in the fabric of the Smart Second Skin Dress releases therapeutic scents, while coloured liquids are carried by a network of medical tubing intended to represent the human cardiovascular system. The release of scent and the movement of the liquids are wirelessly activated by data signals transmitted by sensors worn by the wearer.

50

Japanese architect Makoto Tanijiri
teamed up with Toshiba to create
the Lucéste lighting system shown
here. The ceiling-mounted system
diffuses light through a veil of
swirling mist that mimics the
passage of clouds. The system is
interactive, triggered to change
colour or light levels when users
clap their hands. Lucéste is taking
LED lighting and touch-free remote-
control systems in a new direction.

The Soft Architecture lighting system manufactured by Flos has been created from a new composite material known as Under-Cover Technology. The material enables lighting to be seamlessly integrated with normal plasterboard and a range of other ceiling surfaces. The material also makes it possible to adjust colours and lighting levels to create a soothing atmosphere or a relaxing mood.

throughout the day, as current systems do, but will simulate the rotation of the sun to deliver the appropriate angle of light at the right time of day. Aligned with other environmental controls, lighting could transform the interior into a 'fifth season' of perpetual summer, irrespective of the time of year.

The benefits of channelling natural light into an interior were a source of inspiration for Ross Lovegrove, designer of the Sun Tunnel lighting system for Velux. Rather than use electricity, Sun Tunnel uses the sun as a bulb for a daylight lamp. According to Lovegrove, by integrating sunshine into lighting, the design brings 'a moment of enlightenment into the home'. The system consists of a device on the roof that harnesses the sun's rays and reflects them into the rooms below, where a diffuser allows residents to adjust the intensity and direction of the light. The advantages of Sun Tunnel are two-fold: it creates a better living environment, and makes use of a sustainable source of energy. Sun Tunnel enables residents to enjoy the benefits of natural light in spaces where windows and skylights are not viable, and, in so doing, may also provide them with a means of counteracting health problems associated with insufficient levels of natural light.

Advances in LED lighting have revealed its potential as an expressive medium that could be used to generate atmospheric decor. Toshiba is exploring the possibility of using LEDs to create *akari*, or, as it is known in the West, 'mood lighting'. The electronics firm is developing a unique overhead lighting system that bathes an interior in changing hues of LED light diffused by a screen of swirling clouds. Called Lucéste, the system was commissioned from Makoto Tanijiri, an architect. Its design resembles a skylight through which shifting

cloud formations can be seen. Lucéste's 'clouds' thin out to make the 'sunshine' brighter, or appear to thicken to efface the 'sun' altogether. As it continues to develop atmospheric lighting, Toshiba is demonstrating that future generations of LEDs will do far more than merely brighten rooms.

Sound, like light, is a key ingredient in the creation of a sensory environment. Music stimulates certain parts of the brain, affects motor skills and has been known to impact on heart rate, respiratory rate and blood pressure. Noise, on the other hand, has been proven to have detrimental effects, and, when possible, is systematically filtered out. Future sound systems will be embedded in the very fabric of a building to provide interiors with omni-directional sound emitters, complemented by acoustic surfaces that dampen unwanted noise. Sound-wise, the interior of the future will resemble an anechoic space, enabling the quality of sound to be much clearer than it is today.

Electronics conglomerate Sony is pioneering new methods of integrating sound with furniture, interior decoration and architecture, thus forging new frontiers for interior design. Sony's Monolithic Design concept brings structure and sound together as one. A unique speaker drive system, vertical drive technology, and proprietary digital-signal processing software make it possible to incorporate speakers into a wide range of materials. The technology means that audio signals can be amplified through glass, metal, stone and wood – materials used in both furniture-making and architecture – transforming basic architectural components into invisible sound devices. The use of large-scale transmitting surfaces will result in better sound quality, especially in heavily trafficked interiors subject to several competing sound sources and radio interference.

Although soothing surroundings promote relaxation, the importance of a good night's sleep will always be central to our energy levels and overall well-being. In his design for the bed of the future, Mathieu Lehanneur created a unique environment in which sound, lighting and temperature are as important as the quality of the mattress. Called Once Upon a Dream, the bed was designed for the hotel in Reims, France, owned by Veuve Clicquot, and resembles a room more than it does an item of furniture. Featuring a floor and a ceiling, and surrounded by columns and self-closing curtains, the unit is driven by technology integrated seamlessly into its structure. Before he began the design process, Lehanneur read several psychological studies on insomniacs, and even consulted a sleep specialist. The data he amassed showed that deep sleep is achieved only after passing through several successive stages of sleep, and Once Upon a Dream demonstrates that the application of design skills can accelerate its onset.

When guests are ready to go to sleep, Once Upon a Dream automatically closes its curtains and gradually lowers the lighting levels and temperature. Levels of white noise slowly increase, blocking out external sounds. Low-volume frequencies based on brainwave frequencies are emitted to help subdue neural activity in the brain. By relaxing guests in an environment designed to optimize the conditions needed by body and brain to sleep deeply, Lehanneur's creation practically guarantees a good night's rest. In the morning, the temperature and lighting levels return to normal, and the white noise is switched off, providing a very gentle wake-up call.

Created by French designer Mathieu Lehanneur, this bed automatically encloses users behind curtains, and then gradually lowers the temperature and lighting levels within them. Called Once Upon a Dream, the bed produces gentle levels of white noise to block out external sounds and promote REM sleep. According to the designer, sweet dreams are guaranteed.

REVOLUTIONARY ROOMS

When it comes to futuristic floor plans, fluidity, efficiency and multifunctionality seem to be taking the interior forward. In recent decades, urban apartments have steadily shrunk in size, portending even smaller living spaces in the future. These efficient spaces are likely to integrate several rooms into one, just as cutting-edge apartments and contemporary hotels are doing today. They show how easily washing and bathing facilities can be incorporated into the bedroom, and how kitchen areas can be a focal point in an open-plan interior.

A key blueprint for optimizing the use of living space is the Rotor House concept created by Luigi Colani. The house features a central open-plan area equipped with storage cupboards and an adjacent lavatory. Positioned at one end of this area is a cylindrical revolving unit, which contains a bedroom, bathroom and kitchen in separate sections. Each of the three rooms contained in the revolving unit is the size of a large alcove, and when in position is open to the rest of the interior rather than partitioned off from it. The kitchen and bathroom have had their functional surfaces compressed into an efficient design built into the revolving unit's inside walls. When opened to the interior, the rooms appear to gain floor space as residents make use of the area outside the revolving unit. Because bedrooms and bathrooms are usually unoccupied for most of the day, and access to the kitchen is rarely needed at night, it makes sense to gain space by exchanging one room for another. The Rotor House provides a practical means of storing away living spaces at times when they are not normally used.

Kitchens have long been regarded as the hub of a home, and they are likely to remain so in the future. New kitchen concepts make the kitchen more efficient to use and more sustainable to operate. French eco-design studio Faltazi has created a chicly futuristic kitchen that recycles the waste it generates. Called Ekokook, the kitchen is a sleek, lateral system made up of modular units that contain the sink, cooker and storage cupboards. Each part of the kitchen is equipped with an integrated recycling facility that processes waste at the very point at which it is produced. Waste water is channelled into a filtration tank for recycling as grey water, while food waste is deposited into a compost container, where worms and friendly parasites break it down. Non-biodegradable waste is sorted into individual containers for recycling, while non-recyclable waste is compressed tightly into a disposable cube.

Compact kitchen designs typically offer streamlined alternatives suited to smaller spaces or open-plan areas. Marco Fumagalli's Monoblock kitchen is an efficient design composed of two long, lateral wall-mounted units. The lower unit features a sleek Hanex acrylic surface, a sink, a hob and an oven, while the overhead unit comprises storage cupboards and an exhaust fan. The contours of the lower unit divide the work surface into two different heights, and the overall design brings everything within reach.

The bathrooms of the future promise to be just as compact as the kitchens, and every bit as multifunctional. Japanese bathroom culture is increasingly influencing Western designs, outlining hi-tech visions for the future. Many contemporary bathrooms in Japan are designed to be self-sanitizing and germ-resistant, and future bathrooms will also be fully automated and constructed from

TOP
The space-saving Rotor House designed by Luigi Colani features a cylindrical core that rotates rooms out of range when not in use. Colani has incorporated a kitchen, bathroom, bedroom and living area within a compact unit by eliminating unused space.

BOTTOM, LEFT, CENTRE AND RIGHT
Rotor House has more in common with mobile homes and boats than it does with conventional buildings, being constructed from prefabricated plastic components to make maximum use of limited space. Designed for young couples or individuals, Rotor House presents a blueprint for the compact homes of the future.

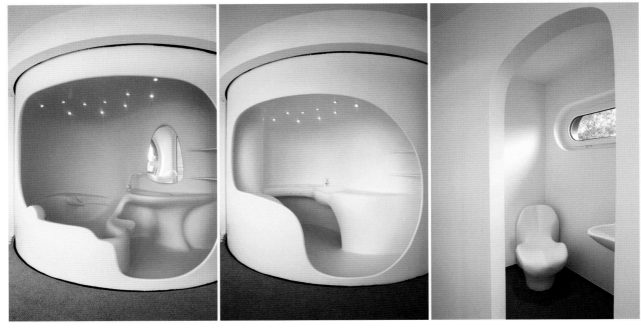

TOP
Naturewash is a waterless washing
machine that uses negative ions
to cleanse nano-coated fabrics.
Designed by Zhenpeng Li, the
device is activated by touchscreen
controls that enable users to clean
their clothes without laundering
them or to refresh them with a
choice of scents.

BOTTOM
With Naturewash, clothes can
even be cleaned and refreshed
without removing them. By sitting
or reclining on the device, users
can clean their clothing in a
fraction of the time it would take
to use a normal washing machine.

anti-odour materials and antibacterial surfaces. Lavatories will be fully technologized, rather like the efficient Washlet designed by Stefano Giovannoni for Toto. The Washlet includes a self-cleaning washing wand, integrated dryer, heated seat, deodorizer and even a remote control. Future showers will feature variable water jets both above and to the sides of the user, and will also incorporate built-in dryers, eliminating the need for towels.

Although kitchens and bathrooms may continue to rely on water for many years to come, most household cleaning will be water-free. Nano-coated objects, including flooring, furniture and

clothing, will be cleaned by a stream of airborne negative ions, which work by binding themselves to dirt particles before whisking them away. The Naturewash device designed by Zhenpeng Li, for example, cleans nano-coated clothing without the use of water or detergent. Rather than submerge their laundry in a tub, users place each item of clothing flat on to Naturewash's horizontal surface, which then cleans or refreshes it (with a grass or flower scent) using negative ions. Users do not even have to remove their clothes: just sitting on Naturewash is enough to make them spick and span.

ABOVE
Designed by French design studio Faltazi, Ekokook is a 'closed cycle' kitchen that converts every element of food and water waste into a fresh resource. The kitchen channels rainwater and waste water through its filters to recycle them, and harnesses wind and solar energy to power its equipment.

PAGES 60–61
In the future, the time allocated to food preparation at home is expected to decrease, and kitchen space is likely to shrink as a result. With this in mind, Marco Fumagalli designed Monoblock, a minimalistic kitchen that makes efficient use of space. The kitchen is constructed from thermoplastic materials and activated by touch technology embedded in its surfaces.

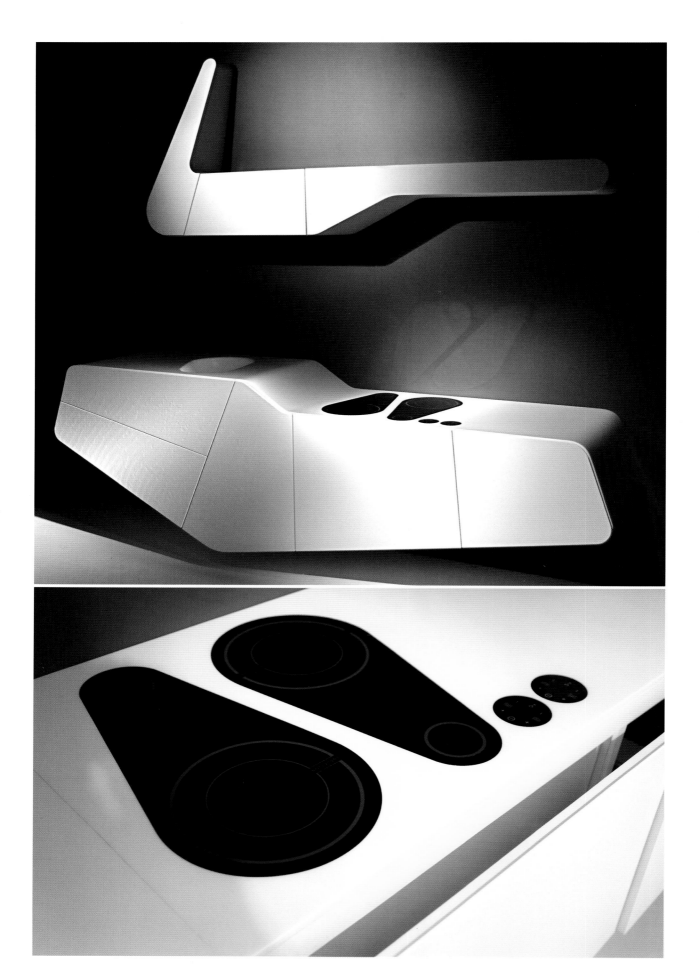

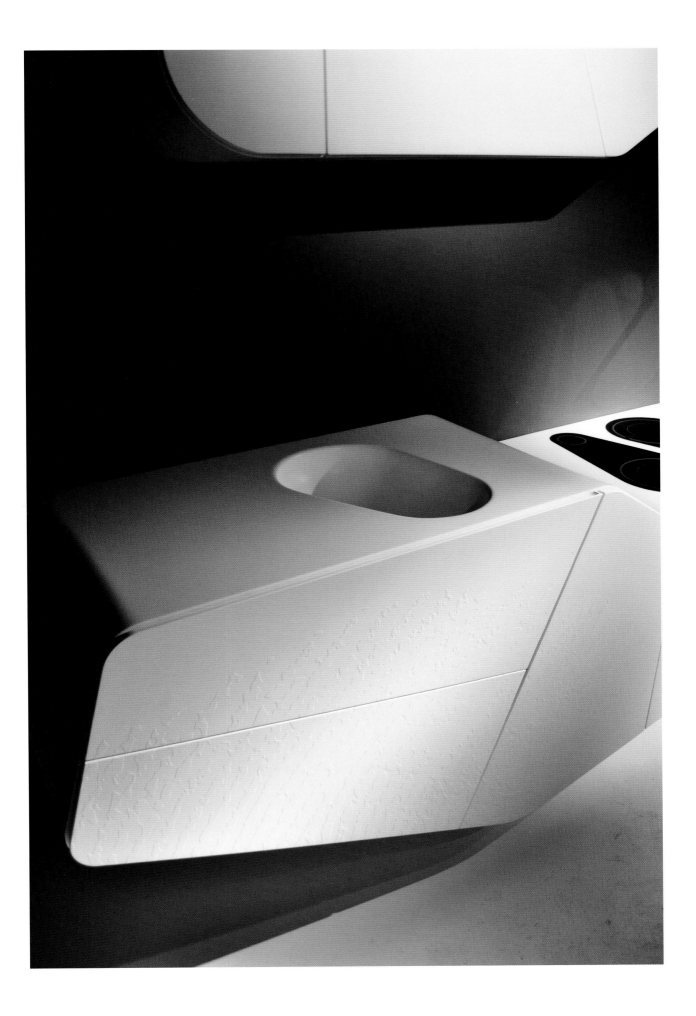

RESIDENT ROBOTS

Artificial intelligence has emerged as a hallmark of future design, a development that promises to change every aspect of the interior. The future home will even be able to construct itself, thanks to robotic building technology capable of fabricating a variety of architectural structures. With such systems as R-O-B, a mobile robotic construction unit developed by Gramazio & Kohler architects in collaboration with Swiss brick manufacturer Keller AG Ziegeleien, building sites can be manned by robots rather than humans. Whereas factories that produce prefabricated homes currently ship standardized components to construction sites, future prefabricators will dispatch robotic units to assemble building materials on site. The technology will also allow unique structures to be built. Mirroring the way in which today's architectural practices hand over their plans to a contractor, the architects and engineers of tomorrow will program robotic machines to construct a wide variety of projects.

Robotic building technology is not limited to assembling materials on site. London-based Italian architect Enrico Dini has designed a robotic building system capable of producing its own construction materials as it builds structures of all shapes and scales. Called d_shape, the system uses 3D printing technology to produce robust, sandstone-like structures from sand and inorganic binders. Dini's system is an all-in-one machine, which means that no cranes, cement mixers, scaffolding or manual workers are needed on site.

The building method employed by d_shape begins with the sand-based construction material, which is processed on site into a liquefied form. Following a structural blueprint, the machine then sprays the material in layers to form the desired structure from the ground up, each layer of material drying and solidifying as soon as it comes into contact with the air. Unlike conventional building methods, which construct the frame first and add architectural components and interior detailing afterwards, d_shape's methodology makes it possible to construct all parts of the structure at once; as the layers are formed, the interior and exterior are created simultaneously. Every aspect of the interior's architecture can be built at the same time as the main structure: staircases, shelving, kitchen units, bathroom appliances and even light fixtures. Because the system's power requirements are remarkably low, and the sand-based construction material is biodegradable, d_shape is an environmentally friendly alternative to conventional construction methods.

The homes of the future will be not only built by robotic systems but also controlled by them. Technologized interiors will develop cognitive abilities of their own, enabling them to perform many tasks independently of their occupants. The robotic technology embedded within such interiors will also be incorporated into household robots able to traverse the living space. These robots will be able to scan their environment, interact with the human occupants and interface with the rest of the interior's technology. American company iRobot, for example, is developing robots that can wash and vacuum floors, clean the pool and mow the lawn. Research indicates that future versions of these household robots will be made in humanoid form. Upright and ambulant, they will be able to mimic some aspects of human behaviour, combining the efficiency of a technician with the friendliness of a concierge.

TOP
Roboscooper, a household robot from WowWee Robotics, is designed to pick up lightweight objects and transport them around the house. When in autopilot mode, Roboscooper scans for unwanted objects lying on the floor and loads them into its tray, ready to take them away. The robot can also be activated by remote control or programmed to pick up and move specific objects.

BOTTOM
Future building sites may be staffed by robots, as engineers and architects create robotic machines capable of constructing buildings. Such systems as R-O-B, the mobile construction unit shown here, are manned by robots rather than humans. Just as the factories of today produce prefabricated homes and ship standardized components to construction sites for assembly, future architects may dispatch robotic units to assemble building materials on site.

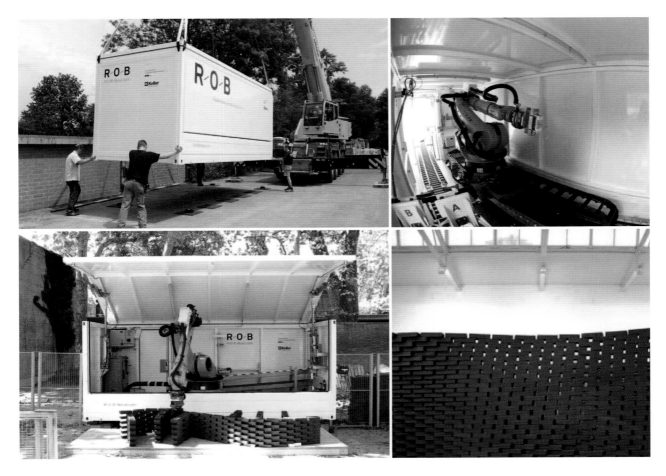

LEFT
The robotic devices produced by iRobot are designed to replace some of the household equipment usually operated by humans. The company has sold more than 5 million home robots to date, including such popular models as the Roomba vacuum-cleaning robot, the Scooba floor-washing robot and the Dirt Dog floor-sweeping robot. Help outside the home can be given by the Looj gutter-cleaning robot and the Verro pool-cleaning robot.

OPPOSITE, TOP AND BOTTOM
French architectural practice R&Sie(n) has created model robots and imaginary robotic landscapes to explore the possibility of integrating robotics into architecture. Its Olzweg project, shown here, paired automated construction processes with cybernetic technology to examine how robots could build and rebuild structures. Future architecture could be designed with mechanical parts and a resident robot capable of maintaining and reconfiguring the space.

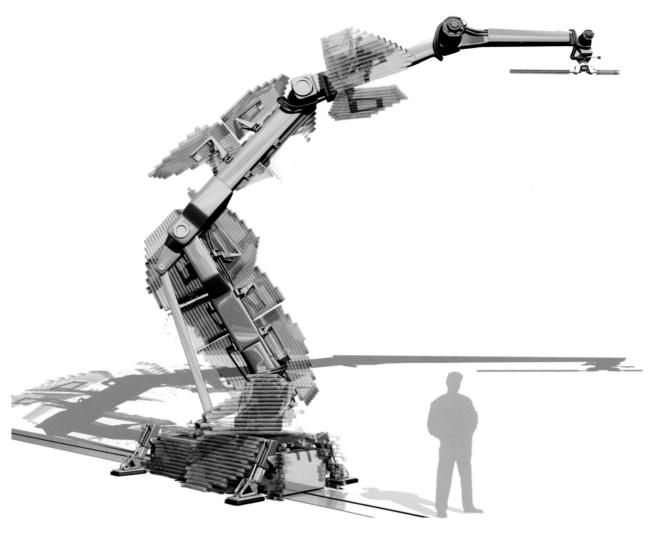

In recent years, 3D printing technologies have attracted the attention of architects and engineers by beginning to demonstrate the ability to construct whole buildings. The d_shape system shown here, created by Italian architect Enrico Dini, uses inorganic binders and such inert materials as sand to build small structures in a wide range of shapes. Such 3D printing technologies are also gaining currency in the aerospace industry, where researchers have recognized that they could be used to build habitats on other planets.

WINKA DUBBELDAM

Since establishing her architectural practice, Archi-Tectonics, in New York in 1994, Dutch architect Winka Dubbeldam has become an influential force in urban architecture. Although her repertoire is vast, Dubbeldam's distinctive style is easy to identify. Her work ranges from residential to commercial, and from virtual to real. Folded-glass façades, integrated technological systems and interactive environments are hallmarks of Dubbeldam's interior designs and architectural projects, which she typically describes in terms of interfaces, skins and sliding surfaces. Her completed projects include large-scale loft renovations and luxury apartment buildings in Manhattan; the fifteen-storey American Loft tower in Philadelphia; and a number of galleries, spas and fashion boutiques across the world. Dubbeldam believes that the static interiors of today are about to undergo a radical change, and in this interview she shares her vision for the 'hyperactive' interiors of the future.

How do you approach interior design today?

I think of the interior as an environment in which the boundaries between technological design intelligence and architecture are blurred. At Archi-Tectonics, our work is focused on researching, rethinking and re-evaluating the current generation of 'performative' models. By that, I mean creating interiors that perform in a non-traditional sense. They will have maintenance-free skins, low-energy appliances and 'green' structures, but also be able to sense and respond to their occupants' needs. So our approach is to foster intelligent relationships between all the different components in the interior by making them sensitive and responsive. And in the wake of advanced digitization, my colleagues and I often need to come up with new modes of fabrication in order to build the shapes and structures we design.

If you were commissioned to design the home of the future, what would it be like?

I would design it like a hyper-modern car, similar to the new Renault DeZir, a two-seater sports coupé. The home of the future would have windows and skylights that open automatically; a satellite sound system with speakers built into padded leather walls; gorgeously sleek electric, reclining, heated leather seating that would appear to levitate above the floor; and discreet storage compartments. The interior would have perforated surfaces rather than hard-edged boundaries, and I would use lighting and graphics to highlight the contours and angles of the architectural components. Door openings would be asymmetrical, and all surfaces would have 'touch' controls.

How would you design domestic amenities and technological systems for the future?

They would be designed to be ultra-efficient, making domestic functions hyperactive. The house's structural centre would be conceived as an armature, *i.e.* a 'smart structure', where integrated cooking, bathing, heating and cooling systems, environmental controls and a central music system would be housed. I'm no longer interested in designing 'empty' aesthetics, where the façade and surfaces are decorated and the core structures are forgotten. My future house embodies an anti-aesthetic, designed from the inside out, not at all concerned with a formal language, and built with added intelligence and performance-driven design.

How will systems like these be constructed?

In future there should be a direct link between the manufacturer and the designer, which essentially cuts out the contractor. With the development of 3D computer software and FTF [file-to-factory] communication, a completely new type of workforce will be created. Designers and manufacturers will team up to fabricate components and come up with bespoke systems for constructing the buildings of the future.

TOP LEFT
This parametric rendering of Dubbeldam's extension for a Manhattan town house shows how the period architecture will remain visible through the contemporary glass façade.

BOTTOM LEFT
This view, looking down into the extension's interior, shows how CNC-milled wood will create a warm texture of natural wood grain.

TOP RIGHT
This sketch shows how Dubbeldam angled the walls of a lakeside house in upstate New York to afford views over the water from every corner. The highlighted section is the 'armature', which places integrated technology and state-of-the-art service equipment in the core of the house.

BOTTOM RIGHT
The continuous glass panes in the completed house reveal how the boundaries between wall and roof were erased to maximize the light and the views. Also shown here is how the kitchen has been integrated seamlessly within the folded walls of the 'armature' behind it.

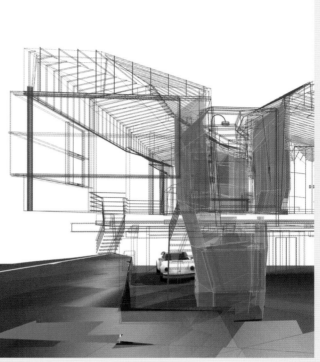

KARIM RASHID

Born in Egypt, raised in Canada and now residing in New York, Karim Rashid has strong feelings about the future, just as he has strong views about products, technology, materials, the human body and design in general. With more than 3000 designs in production, a client base spread across thirty-five countries worldwide and some 300-plus awards to his name, Rashid is one of the world's most sought-after designers. Celebrated for his furniture, metalware and ceramics, he is also renowned for his interior-design projects, including the Semiramis hotel in Athens and the Morimoto restaurant in Philadelphia. Although Rashid roots his work firmly in the zeitgeist, in the following interview he pauses briefly to think ahead and anticipate how interior design will unfold in the future.

If you were invited to design the domestic interior of the future, what would you create?

Our spaces need to be free. Free of history, free of tradition, flexible and customizable. I have designed several 'future' houses over the last few years, making them as inexpensive, democratic, modular and technologically advanced as possible. Objects and systems will work for us, performing tasks and providing multiple functions. Smart materials will become more embedded in our domestic interiors. Polymers – such as synthetic rubbers, Santoprene, neoprene, polyolefin and silicone – and LCD wallpapers and displays are already contributing to this new softness of our interior environment. Materials in our living spaces now flex, morph, and change colour and temperature, and we have heightened experiences via touch. Radiant heat will enable the heating to follow you and not be wasted on the rest of the space, while smart bathrooms will measure our weight and blood pressure and analyse our waste to give us updates on our health. Smart appliances will tell us what is in our fridges and their expiry dates, and even give us recipes based on the food we have at home. Smart closets will have an inventory on our wardrobe to let us know what to wear and create outfits for us.

It's interesting to hear that modular homes may still be popular in years to come. How do you think they will take shape in the future?

I have always been interested in the notion of a modular house, an efficient dwelling that can be erected simply and quickly, that can be inexpensive, democratic and customizable with little cause and great effect. The home I designed for the Smart-o-logic Corian Living exhibition in 2010 gave me the opportunity to develop a modular holistic house for the future – a home that can be produced with a minimal number of concave and convex panels and simple tooling. The soft organic shapes used in the Smart-o-logic home concept create a womb-like structure that is conducive to energy efficiency through the sculptured forms, with no corners to trap hot or cold air. The house promotes a sustainable and smart infrastructure for energy production and consumption and water reuse, and should be built by low-impact construction methods.

How do you think future workspaces will take shape?

Workspaces should be very minimal, perfectly organized, paperless and all digital. I would design spaces that are soft, modular and fluid in their organization and configuration. Systems are needed to help a space expand and contract with the work. There will not be any heavy wooden executive desks or unfriendly conference rooms. The wall surfaces will be covered in LCD polymers to create striking motifs, and they will have technological interfaces. Surfaces could be transparent one moment, and, when privacy is needed, opaque the next. Isolated sound-cancelling systems could reduce noise and replace it with focus sounds.

What can individuals do now to prepare for the future?

My real desire is to see people live in the modus of our time – to participate in the contemporary world – and to release themselves from nostalgia, antiquated traditions, old rituals and meaningless kitsch. We should be conscious and sensorial, and attuned to this world in this moment that we live in.

How do you think future aesthetics will unfold?

The key is the human element, the human scale and the human condition. Design touches us on every level, and continues to define and shape our dimensional interior environments, and create new progressive human behaviours and new languages. Design heightens human experiences and elevates our spiritual well-being, creating space for new experiences. My vision is conceptual, and engages technology, visuals, textures and lots of colour, as well as all the things that are intrinsic to living a simpler, less cluttered, but more sensual existence.

Are sustainable practices likely to lead to better designs?

In the controversial arguments about excess, sustainability and market seduction, I believe that every new object should replace three, and this is dependent on designing better objects for the marketplace. I am trying to use more bioplastic. The biodegradable Garbo rubbish bin is now made of corn, and the Snap chair by Feek is made of 1 per cent recycled polystyrene and 99 per cent air. I am using biodegradable materials in flooring and wall surfaces, and new eco-friendly technologies in the production of goods. Better design for the future means working with new patterns of behaviour and creating new languages, and better spaces mean better experiences, which, in turn, equal a longer life.

TOP
When Rashid produced the Smart-o-logic concept for the Corian Living exhibition in 2010, he designed the furniture and interior architecture as a single expression. This image shows how the anabolic shapes that characterize the furniture and light fixture are mirrored in the surrounding surfaces.

BOTTOM
Rashid's vision of the interior of the future includes sculptural architecture, contouring walls and broad mezzanine levels that afford panoramas over the space. Integrated sound systems, stunning artworks, large-scale screens and small monitors will heighten the sensory appeal of the interior and create a dynamic atmosphere.

MEGA
MATER

STRONGER
BRIGHTER
LIGHTER
SMARTER
SOFTER
GREENER

Interviews with
HELEN STOREY
SUZANNE LEE
MATHIAS BENGTSSON

IALS

New materials can underpin revolutionary innovations or transform everyday objects, shape the environments in which we live, and influence the products we use

Materials may be what make us human. They are the building blocks with which the civilized world was constructed, and the source of the tools that enabled the human race to move forward. Materials sustain local economies and create global commodities, determining how urban environments are built and how human experience evolves. New materials can underpin revolutionary innovations or transform everyday objects, shape the environments in which we live, and influence the products we use. As today's materials become stronger, softer, interactive and more adaptable, they have the capacity to change our way of life more radically than ever before.

Nanotechnology makes it possible to organize atoms and molecules at a fundamental level, revolutionizing the way new materials are designed and structured. The ability to manipulate materials to this degree is augmenting the impact of biomedicine, environmental engineering, energy conservation and product design, and paving the way for more radical innovations in the future. Polymers, when manipulated by nanotechnology, can be enhanced to create hi-tech materials with unprecedented performances. Polymers with nanostructured additives have been used in the production of such materials as shape-memory alloys, security tagging pigments and 'invisible' shielding, enabling them to sense and respond to the presence of pre-programmed triggers.

Materials scientists are also active in the area of metamaterials, in which inorganic materials are developed with performances that seem to defy the laws of nature. Researchers in the field are engineering materials to have a spatial resolution below that of such wave-like phenomena as sound,

light and water. By manipulating materials to resonate outside the conventional wave spectrum, they are able to create new forms of shielding capable of evading detection by most types of sensors.

Materials scientists are likewise active in the fields of artificial intelligence, genetic engineering and biomimicry, where their work has led to such innovations as self-repairing surfaces, 'intelligent' fibres, 'smart' materials and products that contain living, breathing substances. Products made from polymeric materials can be programmed with technological triggers, which, for example, are able to reconfigure the products' shapes and surface textures. Reactive materials, including photochromatic dyes, electroluminescent films, shape-shifting gels and memory alloys, can automatically transform as they adapt to changes in temperature and light levels.

Developments in nanotechnology and advances in polymers have led to the creation of some of the most high-performance materials imaginable. When combined with information technology, they can be used to create the structural networks and technological interfaces that underpin communications infrastructures, and to enhance everyday materials with tiny sensors, software and communications technology capable of sending and receiving data. Lightweight carbon-fibre matrices and sleek metallic meshes are strong enough to be used in the construction of modern buildings, yet soft enough to provide fibres for contemporary fashion. Illuminating skins and pneumatic membranes are as widespread in furniture and interior design as they are in architecture, making materials science a forum

TOP
German designer and engineer Moritz Waldemeyer encrusted the surface of this dress by Hussein Chalayan with crystals and LEDs. Waldemeyer then used electroluminescent wire to connect them to sensors, microcontrollers and video technology, making it possible to display a moving image on the surface of the garment.

BOTTOM
LEDs can be controlled by sensors programmed to transmit data to specific circuits. The data transmissions can create new colours or cause patterns to change shape.

for some of the twenty-first century's most compelling ideas.

This chapter charts what is proving to be a definitive moment in materials innovation by featuring those materials that are forging future directions for the creative industries. As the materials of tomorrow demonstrate new performances today, they are breaking free from conventional categorization, and the sections that follow are structured according to the new aesthetic roles and advanced functions that such materials have acquired. Six sections, titled 'Stronger', 'Brighter', 'Lighter', 'Smarter', 'Softer' and 'Greener', feature materials created through technological breakthroughs, making the world around us lighter in weight, softer in feel and brighter in appearance. The chapter concludes with interviews with Helen Storey, Suzanne Lee and Mathias Bengtsson, who explain, in their own words, what some of the most important challenges for materials science will be in the decades to come.

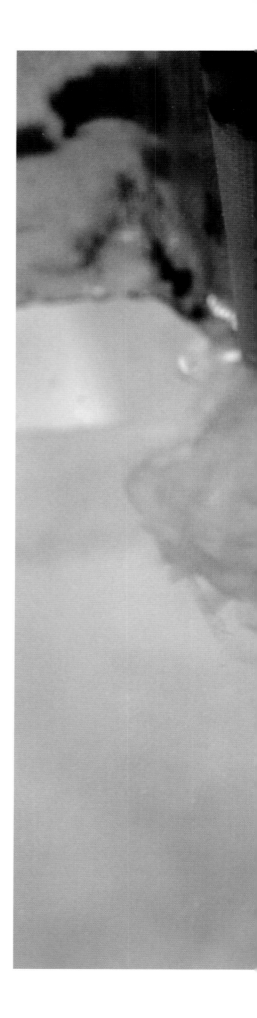

Water-soluble materials tend to break down and biodegrade faster than many other substances, making them an environmentally friendly choice. The research into biodegradable packaging conducted by British fashion designer Helen Storey (see page 118) led her to develop water-soluble textiles that can simply be dissolved when no longer wanted.

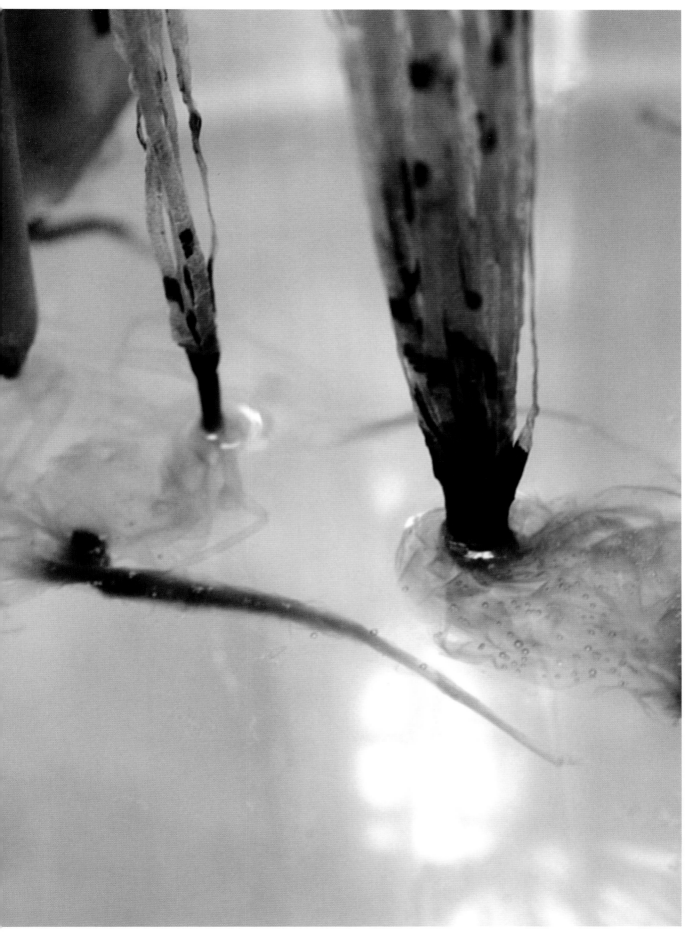

STRONGER

Civilizations are often referred to by the types of materials they used: the people of the Stone Age, the Bronze Age and the Iron Age continue to be characterized by the materials they mastered over time. Future generations are likely to remember our era for the drive to make tough materials even stronger, and for the development of mechanisms that improve the strength of a material while boosting its performance. For decades, the use of hardening systems and the addition of alloys have provided additional strength, but today these methods are being superseded by hi-tech processes that alter the material's microstructure. The incorporation of nanostructured particles and polymeric substances can reduce a material's fatigue and dramatically enhance its strength. It can also improve its ability to withstand impact, as well as heighten its performance when subjected to compressive stress.

Construction materials, such as steel, iron and concrete, are among the strongest used today, but in the future they are likely to be replaced by materials developed for aerospace applications. The resilience of the heavy steel rebar used to build skyscrapers is rivalled by high-tech gossamer filaments strong enough to hoist a satellite into orbit. The addition of nanofibres to composite materials increases tensile strength, making it possible to distribute such materials over larger surface areas without reducing their performance. Today, the strength of a material can also emanate from its surface: the application of coatings, films and solvents produces chemical reactions that both improve performance and heighten the surface's aesthetic appeal. The materials described in the remainder of this section demonstrate surprising durability and unprecedented strength, while the products they can be used to produce promise to last long into the future.

Fordacal

Fordacal is a calcium carbonate compound, and fine grades are used in sealant applications and surface coatings to strengthen their resilience without discolouring any pigments or affecting gloss levels. Fordacal can dramatically enhance the appeal of products, giving them a rich colour and lustrous surface. The compound is currently being used in applications ranging from decorative coatings to product design, but its strength and surface characteristics position it as a future architectural material.

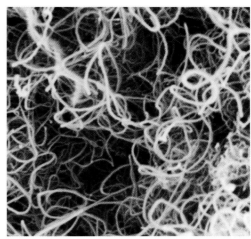

TOP LEFT
Fordacal, shown here in powder form, can dramatically enhance a product's strength and adhesiveness.

TOP RIGHT
Nanofibres can be manipulated at the molecular level to boost the reliability of any product, whether fibre-based or not.

CENTRE
German manufacturing company GKD has developed a method of weaving metal textiles that can measure up to 8 metres (26 feet) wide and 40 metres (131 feet) long. The textiles range in style from large-scale, transparent open weaves to dense, opaque surfaces, while some even incorporate lighting and digital media. The patented, media-equipped stainless-steel mesh shown here was developed jointly by GKD and fellow German company ag4. LEDs and SMDs (surface-mounted devices) integrated into the weave enable the mesh to pulse with colour.

BOTTOM
Called *She Changes*, this sculpture by American artist Janet Echelman is suspended from a massive ring of hollow steel hung between three steel poles of varying heights. It was crafted from Tenara, an architectural material chosen for its resistance to strong winds and ability to retain its red pigment despite constant exposure to ultraviolet rays.

Graphene

Graphene is a single layer of densely packed carbon atoms bonded together in the shape of a honeycomb lattice. The material it creates is formed by tightly stacking individual layers of graphene on top of one another. Graphene's structure makes it superstrong, but also gives it a high degree of electrical conductivity and optical transparency. As a result, it is an excellent material for producing transparent conducting electrodes, which can be used to heighten the efficiency of LCD (liquid crystal display) surfaces, touchscreens, photovoltaic cells and LEDs. As a naturally occurring substance that is conducive to illumination, graphene is being engineered to make the organic photovoltaic cells and organic LEDs of the future.

Inorganic Nanofibres

Nanofibres have emerged as a miracle material, and are being used in an ever-widening range of applications. Although many can be harvested from natural sources, most nanofibres are synthesized from inorganic substances that have been liquefied and subjected to an electrical charge, which forms micro fibres in the fluid. Those known as 'ceramic nanofibres' are formed at high temperatures, and are typically used to craft hard surfaces, sharp edges and products made to withstand heat. Inorganic nanofibres can be used to strengthen many different substances, making nano-based materials ideal for use in protective or high-performance clothing, filters made to withstand chemical agents, footwear and engine parts.

Photopolymers

A photopolymer is a polymer that solidifies when exposed to specific types of light, typically ultraviolet. Because they are extremely strong, photopolymers are the main materials used in rapid manufacturing. Commercially manufactured in powder form, the polymers form objects by being applied in layers, which harden as a light beam is directed on to them. To make the process more sustainable, researchers are currently exploring the possibility of deriving photopolymers from biocompatible sources without compromising their strength.

Flex-Foot is a high-performance prosthetic foot designed for all ages and levels of activity. It is made from carbon fibre, which is both flexible and strong, enabling the user to move quickly and comfortably.
Its manufacturer, orthopedic specialist Össur, uses carbon fibre to give prostheses a level of performance that was previously unimaginable.

Soladyne

Derived from nanostructured PTFE (polytetrafluoroethylene) particulates, Soladyne is used as a coating for architectural fabrics. One of the few coating materials able to withstand heated printing processes and welding, Soladyne makes it possible to apply a wide range of colours, surface textures and motifs to construction materials, leading to design innovations and new aesthetic styles. Soladyne heightens a material's durability, reducing maintenance costs and preventing colours from fading. A Soladyne coating is more durable than most paints, and will last much longer than most other surface coatings.

Ultra-high-density Concrete

Ultra-high-density (UHD) concrete is strikingly resistant to the deformation known as 'creep', the tendency of a hard material to yield to environmental stresses and gradually crack and crumble over time. Projections for a containment vessel for nuclear waste built with UHD concrete indicate that it could last for up to 16,000 years, effectively surviving until after the nuclear contaminants have dissipated completely. The potential of the material is causing architects to re-evaluate the role of concrete architecture. Buildings constructed with UHD concrete will last so long that they promise to be the fossils of the future.

Ultra-high-molecular-weight Polyethylene

Ultra-high-molecular-weight polyethylene (UHMWPE) is the basis for fibres developed especially for use in the human body, some of which have begun to revolutionize surgical procedures. UHMWPE fibres make it possible to shape and sculpt the human body cosmetically, as well as improve post-operative recovery, reduce scarring and simplify difficult surgical procedures. Dyneema Purity, for example, is an incredibly resilient fibre that, weight for weight, is fifteen times stronger than steel, making it ideal for complex, multi-suture applications. Dyneema Purity enables medical-device designers to think beyond the use of such traditional materials as metal and polyester fibres. Whether used in high-impact applications, including sports medicine and joint-tissue repair, or in delicate cardiovascular procedures, the material's high strength, low profile, softness and resistance to abrasion are helping to build the life-enhancing products of the future.

Dyneema Purity is a fibre made from ultra-high-molecular-weight polyethylene (UHMWPE). With a strength-to-weight ratio that can be up to 100 times greater than that of steel, Dyneema fibres are among the strongest materials made today. They can be used to make sports equipment flexible, lightweight and strong, and, being fully biocompatible, have a wide range of medical applications.

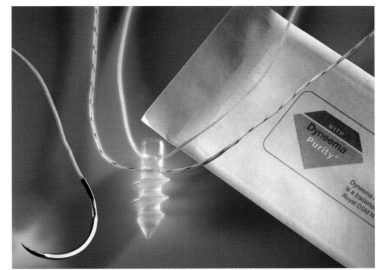

Ultrason

Derived from polyethersulfone (PES), Ultrason is a transparent material with a high degree of durability, strength and heat-resistance. It is resilient enough to withstand temperatures up to 220°C (428°F), enabling products made from it to be sterilized without melting or breaking. Ultrason is impact-resistant and can tolerate high levels of mechanical stress, making it virtually unbreakable. It is proving to be a popular alternative to polycarbonates, and in the future is likely to be widely used in the electronic, automotive and aerospace industries. Ultrason's exceptional strength and resistance to heat mean that it has the potential to replace ceramics and metals in many applications.

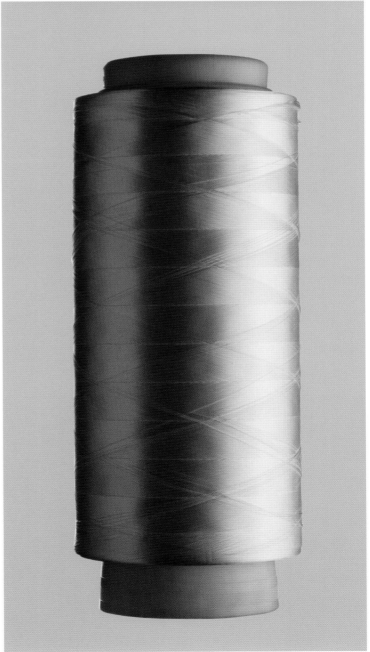

BRIGHTER

Whereas most of the new materials developed in the twentieth century were made with practicality in mind, many of those being produced in the twenty-first are intended to be sources of aesthetic innovation. While scientific breakthroughs have made it possible to create technologically advanced materials, they have also created scope for brighter colours, richer textures, illuminating surfaces and lavish motifs. No longer designed for practical use alone, materials are in themselves playing a key role in taking aesthetics forward.

Materials that react to light can be used to create striking visual effects, while those incorporating optic fibres and capillary arrays can add a degree of luminosity to an otherwise dense surface. Advances in clarifying substances have made many materials more transparent, and colour tints more vivid. Huge slabs of translucent concrete can channel light through solid walls, while tiny crystals are engineered to brighten visual displays. Even glass, one of the most transparent materials, can be made clearer when manufactured with additives or given coatings that direct the light that passes through them. Clear polymers can rival glass in clarity as well as performance, making it possible to produce transparent architectural elements that will lighten and brighten the built environments of the future.

Durabis

Durabis is a clear polymer coating developed by the TDK Corporation; its name is the Latin for 'you will last'. Clear polymers are replacing conventional glass in a variety of applications, from car windscreens to architectural glazing. As surface coatings, they brighten the surface and enable all parts of the colour spectrum to be reflected equally. They can also be used as a layer between two glass sheets, creating unique graphic effects. Clear polymers continue to be engineered for better resistance to heat, and, as they achieve greater flame- and smoke-resistance, they are predicted to replace glass completely.

Liquid-Crystal Helixes

When the pitch of helical liquid crystals is directed, the light they reflect can be channelled in a controlled wavelength. A consortium of researchers based at Philips Research, the Eindhoven University of Technology in The Netherlands and the University of Alberta in Canada is pioneering techniques that make it possible to direct the liquid crystals in three dimensions. The liquid-crystal helixes can then be used to increase the brightness of powered displays without consuming more energy.

TOP LEFT
Milliken Chemical's Millad NX8000 clarifier is highly transparent, effecting a 50 per cent reduction in haze compared with the current industry standard. The product makes some materials so transparent that they appear to be invisible.

TOP RIGHT
Developed as part of a Philips Design research project called SKIN, the Frison bodysuit is equipped with biometric sensing technology that activates a series of LEDs when it detects changes in ambient pressure.

BOTTOM
Stainless-steel meshes with integrated LEDs are emerging as a material of choice for architects. Transparent by day, they can be used to display images across a building's façade by night. Such products as Mediamesh and Illumesh, shown here, are manufactured by GKD and ag4.

LiTraCon

LiTraCon, the creation of Hungarian architect Áron Losonczi, is a combination of lightweight optical fibres and dense concrete. It is usually manufactured in block form, with networks of tiny optic fibres embedded in it. The fibres form a matrix that transmits light from one side of the block to the other, while also intermeshing with the concrete's aggregate materials to reinforce them. Although LiTraCon diffuses light, it still has the strength and durability of concrete. In particular, it has high compressive strength, meaning that it can be safely used for load-bearing structures. Walls made from LiTraCon can be up to 20 metres (66 feet) thick without any loss of light. Although LiTraCon has been dubbed 'transparent concrete', it is not possible to see through it; it is possible, however, to see shadows, movement and light fluctuations.

Millad NX8000

Manufactured by Milliken Chemical, Millad NX8000 is a chemical additive that gives transparent membranes a superior degree of clarity. When added to polypropylene plastic, for example, it endows the material with unprecedented levels of transparency. Millad NX8000 makes it possible to use sustainable substrates in products and packaging without compromising the transparency of the end product. The use of Millad NX8000 in plastics dramatically reduces their toxicity, making it compatible with most industry standards of sustainability.

Polymer LEDs

A collaborative research project carried out by scientists at the University of California, Los Angeles, and the Chinese Academy of Sciences in Beijing has shown that white LEDs fabricated from a new type of conductive polymer can dramatically enhance LED emissions. The polymer is organic, and has mechanical properties that render any light-emitting structures made from it more flexible than those made with inorganic polymers. For example, illuminating substrates and electrodes made from the organic polymer can be sharply bent without breaking. The light emitted by polymer LEDs is stable, making the LEDs suitable for use in large-area lighting displays.

Nancy Tilbury's Bubelle dress, created as part of the SKIN research project run by Philips Design, is constructed from delicate bubble-like forms that illuminate in response to changes in the wearer's body temperature.

TOP
This side view of a clear Sensitile Scintilla tile reveals the light-conducting channels integrated within its structure. These tiny optical pathways transform each tile into an interactive surface that responds to light, shadows and movement.

BOTTOM
Loop.pH's Light Sleeper bedding consists of a programmable duvet and pillowcase that function as an alarm clock. They wake the sleeper by slowly illuminating, mimicking the break of dawn.

Quantum-Dot Composites

Quantum dots are particles of inorganic semiconducting material so tiny that their sizes are measured in nanometres. The particles possess electronic and optical properties, which become more intense as they increase in number. Their optical properties differ from those of luminous materials made from bulk solids. Philips Research is exploring the possibility of combining quantum dots with polymers, in order further to boost their luminescence. Quantum dots have the potential to be used as a form of lighting similar to LEDs, but their colours would be determined by the size of the dots rather than by specific diodes.

Sensitile Scintilla

Sensitile Scintilla are tiles made from transparent or coloured polymer into which small light-conducting tubes have been placed. Thanks to a process described by the tiles' manufacturer, Sensitile Systems, as 'internal reflection', light entering one end of a tube is emitted from the other. Working collectively, the tubes cause the tiles to shimmer and ripple with light in response to moving shadows and changes in light intensity. The tiles can be used to transform ordinary walls and partitions into interactive surfaces. Sensitile Systems has applied the same optical technology to tiles made from resin and concrete.

Transparent Silicone

Liquid silicone rubber is a groundbreaking transparent material. In common with other rubber silicones, it has flexibility and strength, but also an optical clarity so outstanding that it can be used to produce highly complex transparent products. Liquid silicone rubber provides an economical alternative to traditional thermoplastic materials or glass, and is widely used for such optical components as lenses and optical fibres.

Produced by LG Hausys, HI-MACS is a uniquely versatile surface material that can be used to create a wide range of shapes and designs. The Lucent range can also be combined with light sources, as shown here, generating new lighting solutions and giving surfaces a luminosity of their own.

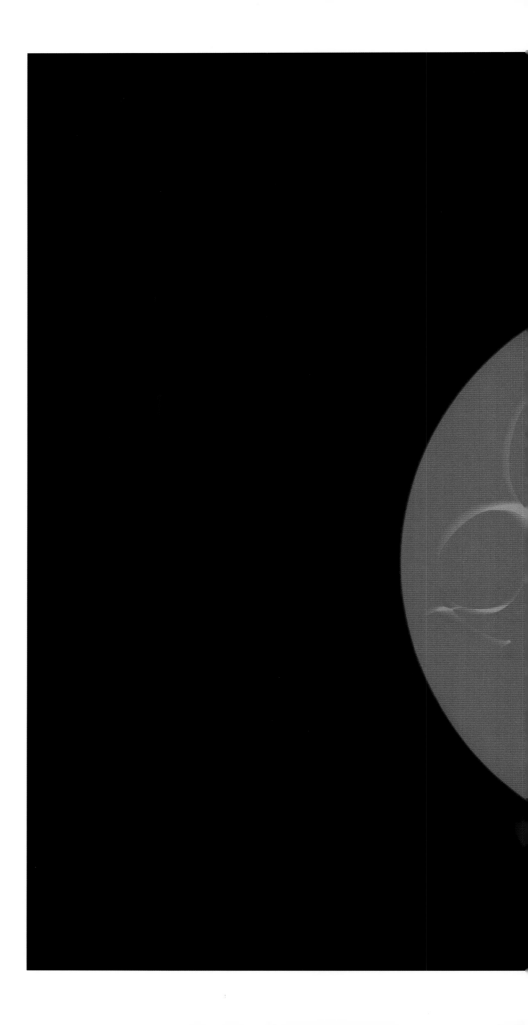

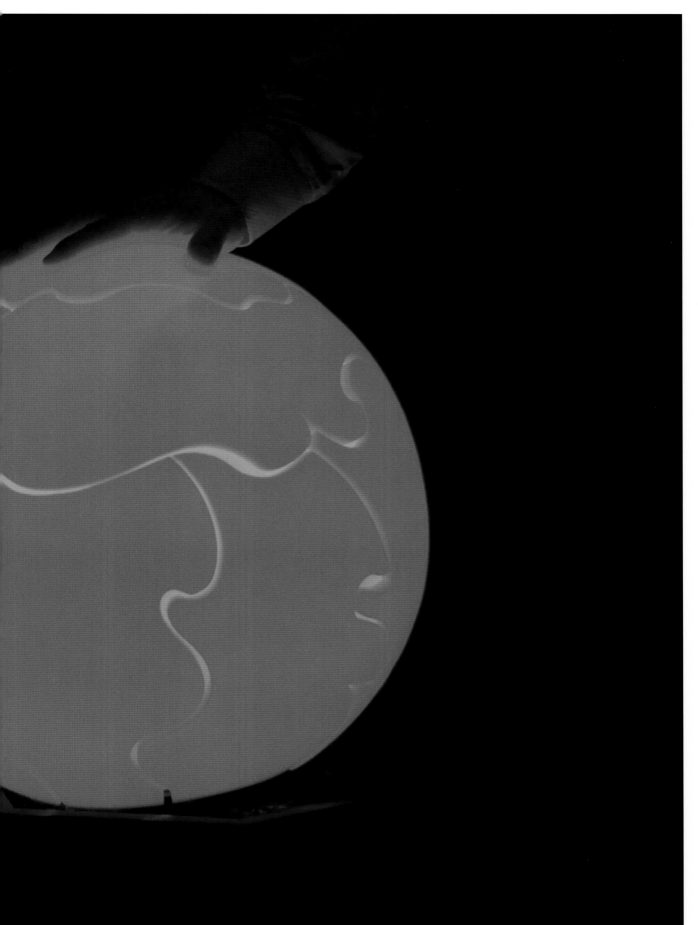

LIGHTER

Robust materials are often equated with density and mass, while lightweight materials, by comparison, can appear flimsy, fragile and weak. Technological developments are reversing this norm, and it is now possible to create superstrong materials that weigh far less than traditional materials with equivalent strengths. Smaller in mass and much lighter in weight, materials derived from polyurethane elastomers, fibre-reinforced polymers, metal alloys and biomimetic substances are heralding a new generation of lightweight designs.

Materials developed for the automotive and aerospace industries include a wide range of metal alloys and high-performance fibres, many of which have found applications in other areas of design. Titanium, typically alloyed with other metals, is often used for applications where high strength and low weight are required, such as the production of lightweight parts for jet engines, spacecraft, medical implants, sports equipment and communications technology. High-modulus fibres have demonstrated unprecedented strength and surprisingly low weight ratios, and although they are flexible, they are also rigid enough to give everyday products structure and shape. Such materials are revolutionizing the way in which products are manufactured, while their low mass will dramatically reduce the energy needed to ship them to the consumer.

Carbon Fibre

Carbon atoms bond together in microscopic crystals that are more or less aligned on a long axis. The alignment makes it easy to extract long filaments from raw carbon, and the microscopic crystals present in the carbon make them incredibly strong for their size. Although a single carbon fibre consists of several thousand carbon filaments, it is extremely lightweight for its strength. Carbon fibres have the strength and resilience of metal fibres of a similar length, but weigh far less than most other strong filaments. Carbon fibres underpin many aspects of architecture and design today, often in surprising guises. Vehicles are partially constructed from carbon-fibre components, aeroplanes are made with carbon-fibre composites and sailing boats are being fitted with carbon-fibre sails. As materials scientists develop new methods of processing carbon, and engineer it to conform to fire and safety regulations, it is revealing its potential to be an essential material for the future.

Concrete Cloth

The use of architectural textiles is rising annually, with applications ranging from commercial and residential buildings to military camps and open-air concert venues. It is likely to be a growth area within the construction industry, in which the use of the groundbreaking cement-impregnated fabric known as Concrete Cloth is becoming more widespread. The creation of Welsh firm Concrete Canvas, Concrete Cloth is pliable and easy to work with, and can be moulded by hand and readily set into shapes. It makes the construction of strong and stable structures simple, efficient and quick.

TOP
Concrete Canvas broke new ground when it developed the material known as Concrete Cloth. Made from fibres impregnated with dry concrete, the cloth hardens to form a solid concrete surface when it is sprayed with water. Its many applications range from the building of retaining walls to ditch lining, as shown here.

BOTTOM LEFT
Lightweight and extremely strong, carbon fibre is an ideal material for sports equipment. Carbon fibres are as flexible as they are durable, acting as shock absorbers in the event of an impact.

BOTTOM RIGHT
The Vienna-based practice Veech Media Architecture has designed a number of inflatable textile structures in response to commissions for lightweight portable architecture. The roof of this dome-like portable textile pavilion was designed with ventricles in the roof to promote the circulation of cool air inside and to enable hot air to escape.

TOP
Working under the name of
Tactility Factory, Belfast-based
textile designer Trish Belford
and architect Ruth Morrow
are pioneering methods of
combining delicate fabrics with
concrete to give the material
a soft, tactile surface.

BOTTOM
Produced by Acoustical
Surfaces, an American
soundproofing company,
the Sound Silencer acoustic
panel shown here is made
from small beads of porous
expanded polypropylene,
a highly versatile and sound-
absorbent material.

Ingeo Biopolymers

Developed by NatureWorks, the Ingeo family of biopolymers comprises lightweight, high-performance fibres that deliver superior strength while weighing significantly less than other industrial fibres. They can be interwoven with other materials to create fabrics for protective clothing, providing the strength and reinforcement of armour for a fraction of the weight. Ingeo fibres blend well with other types of fibre, and are used widely in the fashion industry, with a new generation of designers using fabric made from Ingeo biopolymers to create couture garments and cutting-edge footwear (see page 113). Innegra S, another type of biopolymer, can be woven with fibreglass to produce composites that are lighter and tougher than fibreglass alone, making it an ideal material for use in boat hulls, sports equipment and engine parts.

Octamold

Octamold is a lightweight, load-bearing structural material that can be manufactured from polymers, ceramics, metal or recycled raw materials. With a lattice-like construction, it is made from interlinked octagonal spheres to optimize surface-to-volume ratio. Octamold represents a revolutionary alternative to other composite panels, space dividers and large-scale screens, as tensile, compressive and torsion forces are optimally shared across its entire structure. Octamold can also be fitted with fasteners and other hardware, giving it a wide range of applications, from the automotive and marine industries to furniture design.

Porous Expanded Polypropylene

Porous expanded polypropylene (PEPP) is a semi-rigid, lightweight material with acoustic properties. Whether made into acoustic tiles or moulded forms, PEPP is waterproof, soft, easily coloured and sound-absorbent. The material can incorporate fibres, and responds well to surface treatments. Lightweight PEPP lasts longer than expanded polystyrene, and is easier to recycle, making it a sustainable means of dampening noise.

Recycled Paper

Paper is coming into its own as a construction material. Lightweight, sustainable and biodegradable, paper is replacing heavier materials in the production of drywall, ceiling tiles and insulation. Sustainable paper for interior applications is not made from recycled pulp alone, but combined with fibres from such fast-growing biomasses as hemp. Three-ply, tear-resistant paper with a PET (polyethylene terephthalate) middle layer can rival the strength of most other lightweight, fibre-based materials.

Spider Silk

Spider silk is one of the world's most remarkable fibres. It is lightweight, waterproof, flexible and strong: gram for gram, spider silk is five times stronger than steel. It is also incredibly elastic, capable of being stretched by up to 40 per cent of its length before breaking. Spider silk's ability to absorb and disperse the energy released by an impact makes it durable and tough. Initially, scientists explored its use in a range of lightweight industrial products, such as parachute cords, protective clothing and composite aircraft parts. Recently, its compatibility with the human body has shown that it is also suitable for use in a range of biomedical applications.

Weightless Concrete

While cast concrete can be beautifully smooth and strikingly sculptural, it is also heavy and unwieldy. Ohio CemTech has developed a unique way of producing concrete forms that are a fraction of their normal weight, making it possible to create large pieces without the need to reinforce the floor beneath them. The company's process replaces the core of a cast-concrete block with weightless styrene foam, drastically reducing density and therefore weight. The resulting material looks and behaves like normal concrete, and hardware can be incorporated into the finished form.

The Israeli architect and
designer Noa Haim takes a
whimsical approach to creating
architectural frameworks.
The 'toolkit' Haim devised
for her Collective Paper
Aesthetics initiative contains
a series of A4 paper-lattice
cut-outs that can be assembled
into three-dimensional
polyhedral building blocks.
The construction system and
forms were inspired by the
megastructure concept of
the 1960s.

Although Concrete Cloth, the innovative construction material produced by Concrete Canvas, has many uses, it was originally developed for the shelters shown here. Lightweight and flexible, the cloth is bonded together to form dome-shaped, tent-like structures. Once erected, each structure is sprayed with water and left to harden, resulting in a shelter strong enough to be used as a military bunker.

SMARTER

Many modern substrates have been integrated with technology, and the materials that result are beginning to influence product design more than they are shaped by it. Microelectronic components, circuits and connectors are being fused with materials capable of conducting electrical impulses and transferring information, eliminating the need for unwieldy hardware and bulky external components. Technologized materials will redefine everyday products as mobile, networked devices, placing information technology at the heart of future human activities.

The demand for hi-tech devices is escalating, and the integration of information technology with conductive substrates will give materials an intelligence of their own. Future materials will appear to think, because they will be programmed to react to stimuli around them and trigger appropriate responses. Silicon chips and sensors can be downscaled to minute sizes and embedded alongside plastic-threaded chip carriers and tiny flexible circuit boards. As in the case of most types of programmable hardware, the networks created within these materials can sustain a range of software applications, and can easily adapt to changes in computational and sensing requirements. Intelligent materials are already beginning to prove their merits, and the examples featured in this section are paving the way for a time when materials and technology will become one.

Antimicrobial Polymers

The application of antimicrobial polymers has expanded rapidly in recent years. Antimicrobial polymers kill germs, and their incorporation into implants and biomedical devices lowers the chances of infection. They are already widely used in wound dressings, coatings for catheter tubes and the manufacture of sterile surfaces. Antimicrobial polymers can also be incorporated into such materials as fabric and packaging. When used in food packaging, for example, they are able to combat such bacteria as E. coli, dramatically reducing the risk of bacterial contamination and food poisoning.

eTextiles

Researchers at Stanford University in California have developed an affordable electronic fabric that functions in the same way as a battery. The fabric is saturated in a coloured solution made up of carbon nanotubes to create a fully conductive material. The process mimics the production of paper batteries, but textile versions are much stronger, more durable and even washable. eTextiles have a density of 20 watt-hours per kilogram, meaning that a piece of fabric weighing 300 grams (10 ounces) could store up to three times the power of a mobile-phone battery.

Metamaterials

Metamaterials are types of cloaking device, constructed from membrane-like materials specially engineered to deflect specific radio waves. In order to divert certain frequencies, the materials are constructed from fibrous particles smaller than the wavelengths they are designed to combat. Typically, these particles measure about 100,000 billionths of a metre in width, making them far smaller than a human hair. Scientists believe that, in certain conditions, it may also be possible to engineer metamaterials so that light waves pass round them, leaving no visible trace of the objects they are concealing. In theory, such materials would manipulate the relationship between light and mass to the degree that a concealed object would not even cast a shadow; effectively, it would be rendered invisible to the naked eye.

Microtaggants

Counterfeiting is a growing problem for companies producing high-end consumer goods. The addition of single, small particles or minute quantities of reactive microchemical agents to such goods makes it possible to verify an authentic product at any stage of its lifespan. Each microchemical agent has a specific wavelength, giving each tagged product a unique, traceable ID. The agents have been developed by private independent laboratories specializing in microscopical and microchemical processes. In the coming years, the prevalence of microtagging seems certain to increase interest in the forensic aspects of design.

Nanofibres

Nanofibres can be engineered with many different performances. They can be synthesized with antibodies to fight germs, programmed to detect airborne contaminants, made compatible with human tissue and altered to filter toxic substances. When used as a material for body implants, they can be synthesized with antimicrobial agents to reduce infection, or combined with cells that trigger tissue regeneration. Nanofibres used in sterile textiles contain not only agents that discolour when they detect harmful bacteria, but also antibodies to fight them. Nanofibres can also be incorporated into sensors designed to detect chemical agents, changing colour and shape to signal the presence of airborne contaminants.

Self-Repairing Compounds

Researchers at the University of Southern Mississippi, Hattiesburg, have developed a polyurethane coating that can repair its own scratches when exposed to sunlight. The coating consists of a mixture of chitosan (a substance derived from the exoskeletons of crustaceans) and the polymer used in the outer layers of a car's paintwork. When the coating is scratched, the chitosan is exposed to the ultraviolet component of sunlight, and responds by forming chemical chains with other materials in the coating, eventually filling in the scratch. When applied to products requiring a protective surface, such self-repairing compounds could minimize maintenance, saving money and labour and reducing waste.

Shape-Memory Materials

Shape-memory materials are 'superelastic' metals engineered to change shape in response to changes in temperature. Such materials as Nitinol can morph into a pre-programmed shape at a designated 'transformation' temperature, and then revert to their original form when the temperature rises. Many shape-memory metals have an extraordinary ability to withstand pressure and compression, making them suitable for use as construction materials or in furniture design. They are also compatible with the human body's physiology, giving them great potential as medical implants and surgical devices.

TOP, LEFT AND RIGHT
Electronic textiles can heighten a garment's performance in many ways. Some can incorporate information technology, or function as communications devices. Pressure-sensing material, such as the quantum tunnelling composite (QTC) fabric by UK firm Peratech, enables clothing to become rigid on contact with another object in order to protect the wearer from injury.

BOTTOM LEFT
Fabric woven with strands of glass and polymer fibres can transmit light and colour.

BOTTOM RIGHT
The new breed of nanofibres includes those that are self-braiding. Such nanofibres can be used to create substances that can change their optical properties or store energy and release it on demand. Like all nanofibres, they are engineered to have diameters of less than 1000 nanometres.

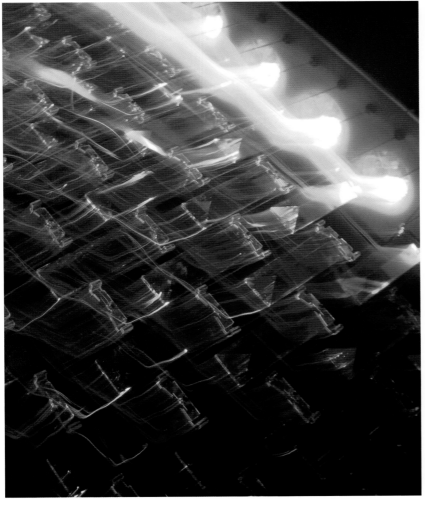

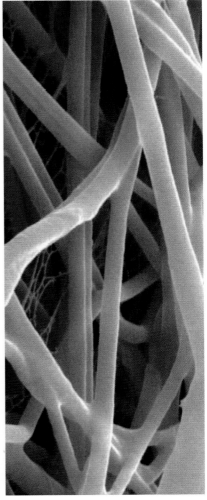

Smart Plastics

Robert Langer, a professor at Massachusetts Institute of Technology, is pioneering a new type of plastic that can change from one shape to another. Like a flower that opens when facing the sun, the plastic morphs into a new shape when illuminated with light at a specific wavelength. This kind of 'smart plastic' has potential applications in a variety of fields. Any goods made from it could be 'shrunk' for easy storage, or scaled to different sizes as needed. Surgeons could insert a string made from the plastic into the body through a tiny incision. When illuminated by light transmitted from a fibre-optic probe, the string could morph into a corkscrew-shaped stent to keep blood vessels open.

Smart Sponge

AbTech Industries' groundbreaking Smart Sponge technology is combating water pollution through its ability to absorb spilled oil. The Smart Sponge soaks up oil without absorbing water, making it a safe and convenient means of removing the pollutant from the environment. The Smart Sponge's unique molecular structure is based on innovative polymer technologies that are chemically selective to hydrocarbons. As the sponge absorbs oil, it converts it into a stable solid for easy recycling. Able to float in both calm and rough water, the sponge remains buoyant even when saturated with oil.

TOP
Developed by German designer and architect Jürgen Mayer, this thermochromatic bedlinen responds to the sleeper's body heat. The warmth of the sleeper leaves a temporary impression on the fabric in the shape of his or her body.

BOTTOM LEFT
The knitted microtube shown here was produced by Australia's Commonwealth Scientific and Industrial Research Organisation (CSIRO), which develops biocompatible 'smart' fibres for neural repairs that accelerate the regrowth of human tissue.

BOTTOM RIGHT
Electronic circuits, sensors and connectors can be produced in many forms today. When scaled down to micro sizes, made from fibres and printed on to wafer-thin substrates, they can more easily be adapted for use in smart materials.

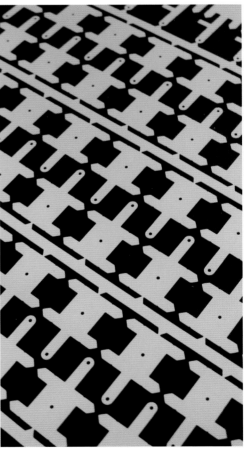

SOFTER

The cutting edge in materials innovation is not sharp, but sensuous and soft. These days, such materials as nanogel, magnetic gel and liquid silicone are providing soft textures and tactile shapes that can dissolve hard edges and soften rigid forms. The elasticity of materials and the versatility of form are essential components of creative freedom, and softer forms give designers more scope to realize their ideas. Soft materials can make products lighter in weight and more elastic in feel, imbuing them with enough flexibility to bend, compress and expand, yet return to their original shapes. When scaled up to architectural proportions, such flexible materials as bendable concrete, inflatable membranes and woven metal mesh become popular alternatives to bricks and mortar, making the built environment appear more sculptural. Just as these new materials were engineered to promote softer shapes and contouring silhouettes, they were also developed with the volume and strength required to support them.

Although surfaces are an integral part of a product, they are often conceived as a separate part of it. The development of multidimensional materials, which have the same properties at their core as they do at their surface, has enabled designers to conceive structure and surface as one and the same. When a single material can automatically shift from thick to thin and from tight to loose, it can mould itself to other components or automatically redistribute strain throughout its entire structure. Such soft substrates can also act as shock absorbers, enhancing a product's durability by absorbing impact energy rather than reacting to it. Soft materials herald a dynamic future for all kinds of design, seamlessly combining the technologies of texture and touch with high performance and elasticity.

The soluble membrane developed by Professor Tony Ryan of the University of Sheffield and fashion designer Helen Storey is soft enough to be worn on the human body, yet durable enough to be made into bottles (see also page 118). When no longer needed, the material dissolves in hot water to form an artificial compost in which seeds can be propagated.

Inflatable Membranes

Inflatable forms can be made from a range of polyester, nylon and PVC materials. Their seams are heat-bonded to create strong structural cells, into which pressurized air or gas is then pumped. With their high degree of elasticity and tactility, inflatable materials are changing the way in which buildings are designed and constructed. They enable architects to design temporary, lightweight, tensile buildings with complex geometries and striking contours. Such buildings can be assembled quickly and easily, in a variety of locations, and then effortlessly taken down, shrinking to one-tenth of their expanded size when deflated. Supported by steel lintels, they can be used as portable outdoor architecture, or as indoor pavilions, providing a uniform backdrop for exhibitions and events.

Liquid Silicone

Liquid silicone has a low viscosity, enabling it to be pumped through pipelines and tubes. With many types of product manufacturing likely to take place in the home in the future, researchers are considering the possibility of supplying liquid silicone directly to domestic replication machines through a house's plumbing. Currently, most 3D printing devices use powdered materials to create rigid objects with hard surfaces, but the use of such materials as liquid silicone will allow future replicators to create soft products. Pigments and other additives can be added to the silicone before it is moulded into shape and vulcanized.

Magnetic Gel

Silicone's ability to form strong bonds and withstand high temperatures has made it a popular choice for a number of industrial and architectural applications. Recent developments have made it possible to mix silicone with magnetic neodymium iron boron particles, creating a soft, pliable material that will stick to steel and to itself. The applications for this 'magnetic gel' are limitless, as the strength of the bonds it forms is such that it can be used instead of hardware fasteners. In interior decoration, for example, the gel could be used to hold in place such items as cushions, curtains or carpets, while also making it easy to detach them.

Nanogel

Translucent nanogel is a remarkably soft insulating material, capable of diffusing light and absorbing sound. In glass insulation systems, for example, the nanogel is squeezed into inter-pane cavities, filling gaps of any size or shape. When combined with other architectural materials, nanogel provides a flexible, lightweight filling that makes them more energy efficient and lighter in weight, while also reducing glare and resisting mould and mildew.

TOP
Researchers at the University of Michigan have developed a new flexible concrete composite known as bendable concrete. The material can be bent into a U-shape without breaking, and can even self-repair any cracks or breaks it experiences. As the material reacts with rainwater and carbon dioxide, it produces calcium carbonate, a compound that expands and fills any cracks.

BOTTOM
Air has emerged as a 'material' of choice for designers and architects alike. When harnessed within airtight membranes and subjected to pressure, air possesses both mass and strength, yet retains a soft, cushion-like quality.

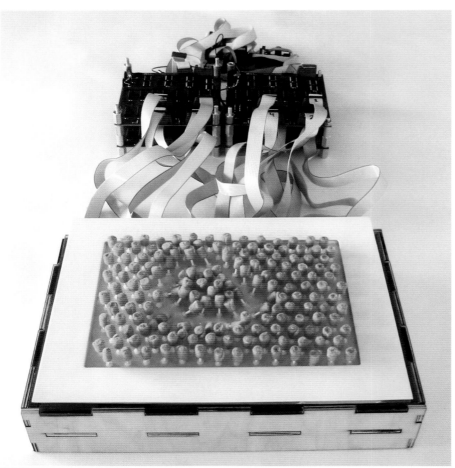

Developed by Hayes Raffle,
Mitchell Joachim and James
Tichenor, super cilia skin (SCS)
is a touch-sensitive interface
that can detect movement and
mimic it. An SCS surface could,
for example, propel objects
across itself by undulating the
fibres in the same direction,
in the manner of the movement
of a centipede's feet.

Soft Concrete

Polymer additives and delicate fibres are changing the performance of concrete, reinventing it as a soft surface material that can bend and flex. Researchers at the University of Michigan are engineering concrete with flexible properties that enable it to mimic the performance of industrial plastics. Bendable concrete has the look and texture of conventional concrete, but is 500 times more resistant to cracking, and up to 40 per cent lighter. The fibres are evenly dispersed throughout the concrete, constituting about 2 per cent of its volume. As a result, bendable concrete can also be classified as a composite, taking a traditional material in a new direction.

Super Cilia Skin

The invention of a new multimodal digital material covered with an array of touch-sensitive fibre-like actuators promises to provide technological interfaces with new types of tactile control. This new material can track movement and touch in one area, and relay it to a variety of separate, but interconnected, actuators. Known as super cilia skin (SCS), the material is essentially a technologized surface based on the fibre-like cilia strands found in the cells of many organisms. Cilia move in undulating, wave-like configurations, transferring information to one another. Collectively, they constitute an actuated, sensory interface, which is exactly the role that SCS plays between technological devices and their environments.

Super Silicone

New polymer additives are creating new grades of silicone, making the material not only stronger and more flexible but also softer and more tactile. One of the most innovative applications of 'super silicone' is the interactive Squish rubber sink designed by Joel Hoag, which features soft sides and a flexible rim. The sides can be rolled up or down to change the height and depth of the basin. Super silicone has the potential to make the bathroom a safer environment by eliminating hard edges and corners, which someone could fall against. In addition, because silicone is non-porous and virtually chemically inert, very few substances stick to it, making it easier to clean.

GREENER

The distinctions between nature and culture are not sharply drawn. Boundaries between the hi-tech materials of the modern human and the organic processes of the natural world are starting to shift as mankind learns how to mimic nature. A new breed of materials is emerging from natural substances, with plant fibres, flower fragrances and organic matter replacing a number of chemical compounds. Biopolymers, which are produced by living organisms, are providing sustainable materials for use in healthcare, agriculture, packaging and food preparation. Natural resins are providing organic additives and binders for pigments, paints and dyes, giving the colour spectrum of the future a decidedly green tint.

The development of a new material brings with it risks and uncertainties; it could fail to perform, discolour, create a chemical reaction or disintegrate over time. The science of biomimicry makes it possible to replicate some of nature's models in new types of material, giving materials scientists a proven track record on which to build. Synthesizing materials from natural forms makes it easier to predict how they will biodegrade and to evaluate their impact on the environment. As materials scientists begin to unlock the secrets of nature, new horizons for eco-friendly materials are beginning to emerge.

Anti-pollution Microbes

Researchers at the University of New South Wales in Sydney are using bacteria to combat air pollution. They have discovered that certain pollution-eating microbes are capable of converting carbon emissions from vehicles and manufacturing plants into pure oxygen. Specimen microbes were harvested from a centuries-old church in Brazil, where they were found growing on the walls. When researchers realized that the microbes were able to consume the volatile compounds found in liquid fuels, they devised plans to embed them in air-filtering systems used in road tunnels. As the microbes digest the traffic-fume toxins, they convert the pollutants into oxygen and water.

Biodegradable Plastic

The disposal of plastics has created numerous environmental concerns, as the process can release harmful compounds. The new generation of biodegradable plastics is made to decompose naturally by biodegrading into the soil: microorganisms metabolize the waste plastic, and produce an inert, humus-like substance similar to the decomposed plant matter that occurs naturally in most environments. Some types of plastic are made from bio-active compounds, including agents that swell when combined with heat and moisture. These agents cause the plastic's molecular structure to expand, enabling the plastic to be broken down more easily.

Biomimetic Materials

One of the first researchers to recognize nature's ability to provide sustainable solutions was Janine Benyus, an American science writer. Benyus coined the term 'biomimicry', from the Greek words *bios*, meaning 'life', and *mimesis*, which means 'imitate'. Since then, the scientific field known as biomimetics has flourished, spawning numerous sustainable materials. Strong glue derived from the compounds that anchor mussels to underwater reefs, fibres coloured permanently without the use of pigments or dyes, fabrics that mimic shark skin, and non-stick coatings based on the lotus flower's stain-proof petals are just some of the materials inspired by nature's know-how.

Biopolymers

Although still very much in their infancy, biopolymers have the great advantage of being raw materials that can be grown rather than extracted, offering an annually renewable resource: as long as you have fertile soil, some rain and the sun, you can produce these polymers. Eventually, most polymers will probably be produced in this way; and given that biopolymers are also biodegradable, their production becomes a sustainable, cradle-to-cradle-type process, with the disposed-of material being used to fertilize the new crop.

Curran

Curran is a high-strength biofibre produced from biodegraded carrots. Nanofibres that occur naturally in carrots are extracted from the decomposed vegetable and bonded with high-performance resins to produce a tough, durable material. The brainchild of biotech company CelluComp, Curran can be moulded into a variety of shapes with varying degrees of stiffness, strength and weight. The material's remarkable characteristics make it an ideal substitute for synthetic fibres that lack sustainability. For example, the fibre's rigidity rivals that of carbon fibre, making it a cheaper and greener material for the production of fly-fishing rods, snowboards and automotive parts. Curran is regarded as more sustainable than carbon because carrots are a renewable resource, and the oils used to produce carbon fibres are not.

TOP
Italian manufacturer Fashion
Helmet produces hand-crafted
motorcycle helmets. Its self-
descriptive Ingeo Helmet
shown here was created as
part of a collection of fashion
accessories made from
materials that are both hi-tech
and environmentally friendly.

CENTRE
This bowl-like form is
made from the bacterial-
cellulose material developed
as part of the BioCouture
research project directed by
Suzanne Lee (see page 120).
Although the material was
intended to be used for
clothing, it is beginning
to find other applications.

BOTTOM
These sleek photovoltaic panels
are a much greener option for
large-scale power grids than
the bulk-silicon and rigid solar
cells they are beginning to
replace. Photovoltaic filaments
are lightweight and efficient,
and can even be spun into
conductive threads to provide
power sources for wearable
technologies.

The EcoKimono, created as part of the BioCouture project, shows how biodegradable bacterial-cellulose material can be used to make lightweight fashion items. Here, the material has been printed with a repeating pattern, revealing that it has much in common with fashion textiles.

Halloysite Nanotubes

Composed of hydrogen, aluminium, silicon and oxygen, halloysite nanotubes are formed naturally in the Earth's crust over millions of years. They are microscopic, typically measuring less than 100 nanometres in diameter, and between 500 nanometres and 1.2 microns in length. Because their hollow centres can hold substances for long periods of time without breaking down, nanotubes are used in medicines and skincare products designed to work continuously. Scientists and researchers are developing methods of processing them for use in numerous commercial applications, including medicine, cosmetics, fragrances and agricultural products.

Pebax Rnew

Pebax Rnew is an elastomer derived from plant-based materials. Arkema, its manufacturer, uses molecules from organic sources, such as the castor oil plant, rather than those from fossil fuels. Since the castor oil plant is inedible and not normally grown agriculturally, its cultivation does not compete with food production. With inorganic materials making up only 5 per cent of Pebax Rnew's total composition, it provides a sustainable alternative to other elastomers used in manufacturing. The material is already in use in the areas of sports equipment and footwear, where it is replacing fossil fuel-based products. In addition to its environmental credentials, Pebax Renew has better temperature resistance and elasticity than many other elastomers.

Photovoltaic Material

Thin-film photovoltaic (TFPV) cells are made by coating solar cells with thin layers of microcrystalline photovoltaic material. The photovoltaic material's efficiency is central to the ability of the solar cells to convert sunlight into energy. Such companies as First Solar, DuPont and SunPower are recognized for advancing the absorption capability of the material, meaning that less of it is needed to generate the amount of energy required. The creation of an efficient, cost-effective supply of photovoltaic material is essential not only to making it accessible to wider sections of the public, but also to providing an affordable alternative to fossil fuels and centralized electricity grids.

HELEN STOREY

Helen Storey is a British fashion designer, but it is not easy to describe her approach to clothing. Many of her designs straddle the divide between tradition and innovation, or bridge the distances between fashion and such disciplines as art, architecture, science, technology and new media. Storey's designs have been made using a wide variety of materials, from natural fibres, latex, plastics and rubber to the PVA (polyvinyl acetate) material she is pioneering today. Collaborations with Tony Ryan, a professor of chemistry at the University of Sheffield, and Trish Belford at Interface, a research centre at the University of Ulster, have led to the development of a range of environmentally friendly 'intelligent' materials with applications in packaging, product design and fashion. In the following interview, Storey shares her current vision for a new generation of materials that sense when they are no longer needed, and automatically dissolve and biodegrade into substances capable of growing new forms.

How did you become interested in creating new materials?

I had been commissioned to work on a packaging-design project and felt as if I was coming to a creative dead end. I had started to read a book about quantum mechanics – the exchanges between energy and matter have always fascinated me, and I wanted to find out more about them – and suddenly the idea of making 'intelligent' packaging that could dematerialize came to me.

What are the applications for materials that can dematerialize?

I started with the idea of making a bottle from materials that would have an intelligent relationship with its contents and automatically disappear when it was empty. Think of a shampoo bottle that disappears when the last drops are squeezed out, or a 'drink me – shrink me' bottle that morphs into a tiny compostable ball when all the liquid has been poured out. Eventually, some prototype 'dissolving bottles' were made that dissolve under hot water to form a gel in which seeds can be grown. This kind of packaging could revolutionize design, radically change the fashion industry and provide a solution to some issues surrounding waste plastic.

What is the material made of?

It is essentially a pre-existing PVA, a water-soluble synthetic polymer, that we adapted for our use. It can be made into a substrate similar to cling film and used in the same way as fabric or plastic, then breaks down completely when it comes into contact with water. The prototype bottles we made could not contain water for very long, but they can hold liquids like shampoo and washing detergent that have a viscous structure.

Can the dissolving materials be used in fashion design?

Yes, they can, but not quite yet. Trish Belford used the material to make dissolving textiles, and series of disappearing dresses were made from them. The dresses were exhibited publicly, hung from scaffolds and gradually lowered into giant vats of water. The material dissolves in water, so when the colourful dresses made from it began to break down, it created a vibrant firework-like show underwater. So far, the dresses made from the material are not for wear; they are meant to be a metaphor to spark discussions about the environmental sustainability of our current fashion industry and what happens to used clothing.

When is the material likely to be ready for manufacturers to use?

Once we've resolved some practical issues, it should be possible to produce the material at an affordable cost. At the moment I'm in dialogue with Unilever, who are considering how the material can be combined with other technologies, and how substances such as dyes will affect it. We also want to see if there is potential for the material to be used as a compost-like soil substitute after it dissolves.

Materials science and fashion came together in Storey's Wonderland project, which culminated in a collection of ten 'disappearing' dresses. The dresses were exhibited in public spaces, where they were lowered into vats of water. Over a period of several days, visitors could see how the dresses dissolved. Storey's project revealed how fashion designers and scientists can collaborate to produce biodegradable materials that make garment production more environmentally friendly.

SUZANNE LEE

From her base in London, Suzanne Lee directs the BioCouture research project, which she started in 2004 with David Hepworth, a scientist and co-director of CelluComp, but runs today with the assistance of scientists at Imperial College, London. By cultivating harmless bacteria that bond active enzymes and cellulose fibres into a textile-like material, Lee and her fellow researchers developed a plant-based membrane without using any man-made derivatives. Lee fashions the material into prototype garments intended to initiate sustainable clothing designs that would be eco-friendly at every stage of their production. As she strives to create clothing that can actually grow itself, Lee recognizes in the following interview the wider potential for biological materials grown by microorganisms to change all aspects of design radically.

In what ways can biomaterials be regarded as materials of the future?

We have reached a point where designers can no longer ignore their responsibilities with regards to sustainability. It's not plausible any more just to create more and more stuff and not think about the product's life cycle. Waste and how to get rid of it have become global issues. That said, there is huge potential for biologically based materials that make use of agricultural waste and microorganisms that can grow materials for us. By literally designing an organism to produce something for you, you can ensure that you build in only the qualities you desire, such as when and how to biodegrade. This method of biomaterial production is super efficient – there is no waste.

What are the future applications of biomaterials?

The sky's the limit: anything from biodegradable packaging to the space industry. Biomaterials will increasingly enter and envelop our bodies and mediate our environments. Medical, product design, textiles, automotive, furniture, architecture, fashion – I see no reason why there won't be applications in all industries. In addition to 'single'-fibre materials like ours, there is a whole emerging world of composites that can add incredible additional functionality. So, for example, we might add a rubbery polymer to give something elastomeric qualities, or use one of the many hemp-based fibres as a substrate to stabilize it.

Do you think future design will be led by materials, or vice versa?

I think the development of new materials will enable us to design – and manufacture, since the two can be inextricably linked in biology – things we might not previously have imagined; and that our relationship with materials will inevitably become more embedded. I think designers are by nature curious and tend to seek out the latest thing, so chances are it will be a combination of designers seeking out materials with interesting new qualities and scientists perhaps having more public dissemination of their work, so the two might connect.

Is interest in biomaterials advancing rapidly today?

In the last couple of years I've seen enormous growing interest from design courses educating the next generation of designers to open their minds to the kinds of materials and methods that scientists are engineering. At Central Saint Martins College of Art and Design, where I'm based, we now need investment or sponsorship from industry to support the kinds of dynamic, stimulating design–science collaboration that will fuel the future economy. BioCouture's current use of the material is only one of the many applications for biomaterials. There is a lot of interest in the biomaterials that are being engineered for use in the human body – a huge and lucrative field. Then there is the whole field of bio-based materials, and also biomimetics [see pages 114, 130], the use of biologically inspired processes and materials.

How do you actually create your biomaterial?

The BioCouture membrane is grown in a tea-and-sugar solution using a microbial culture. As the bacteria synthesize the sugar, they release compounds that gradually form cellulose fibres. When the membrane is extracted and dried, the microorganisms are deprived of their nutrients, meaning that they become dormant, but not dead. The dried membrane behaves like a non-woven textile, and can be pattern-cut in the same way as conventional fabric, dyed, layered, printed and sewn. At the end of its life cycle, the garment can be composted just like any organic food product.

Where is BioCouture heading?

One of BioCouture's long-term ambitions is to grow ready-formed clothing by immersing a garment mould in a vat of liquid containing the bacteria. The bacteria would attach themselves to the mould, assume its shape and mesh themselves into a single, seamless membrane. Once the membrane had been removed from the mould and dried, it would be ready to wear.

TOP, LEFT AND RIGHT
The BioCouture research project directed by Lee uses a bacterial-cellulose material to produce clothing. When dry, the material can be cut and sewn together to form such garments as the indigo-dyed 'denim' and leather-look jackets shown here.

CENTRE, LEFT AND RIGHT
The bacterial-cellulose material can be engineered to produce a range of styles, including this fitted fashion top.

BOTTOM
Grown in vats of a tea-and-sugar solution, bacterial cellulose consists of chains of glucose joined together in repeating units that build up to form microfibres. As the bacterial cellulose dries, these fibres form layered sheets of material.

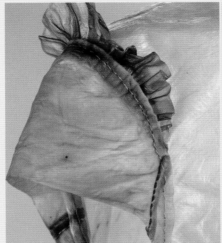 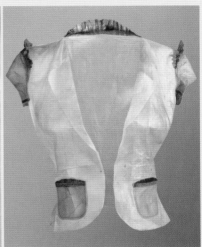

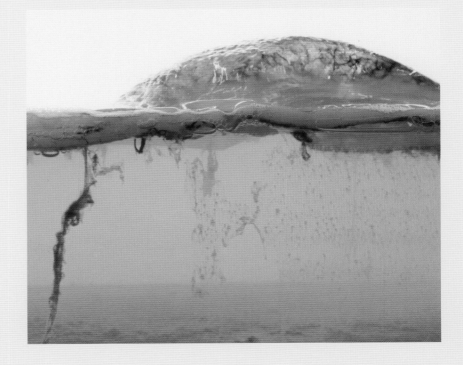

MATHIAS BENGTSSON

The work of Danish designer Mathias Bengtsson is the result of his experiments with materials, processes and technology. His pioneering approach to carbon fibre and paper, for example, has resulted in some groundbreaking developments, and, over time, his furniture has revealed new potential for the materials. In particular, it has shown that they can be used to create designs that combine surface, structure and suspension in a single form, eclipsing the need for additional supports or padding. In the interview below, Bengtsson shares his thoughts on some of the future uses of both materials.

Why are so few furniture designers using carbon fibre today?

The furniture industry has been conservative for many years, and is generally slow to implement new technologies, methods and materials. Recent rapid advances in technology are placing new demands on manufacturers to follow or reflect the new materials of our time, which hopefully will lead to more widespread use of carbon fibre and new materials in general. Bear in mind that issues around carbon fibre's recyclability, maintenance and midlife repair will need to be resolved before it can be considered a viable material for the future.

Will future design be led by materials?

Materials led design in the past, but the future will be different. It is technology that dominates all today's developments, not materials. Technology shapes our time and solves our problems, and it will have more impact on future designs than materials will. Technology will create new ways of designing structures. If you consider how DNA can be manipulated to create 'designer babies', you can see the potential for a set of artificially created structures that mimics the way nature grows and evolves in response to problem-solving. Science can borrow principles from nature to solve problems, grow body parts, create substances that eat oil spills and even convert carbon dioxide to oxygen in the oceans. One day I want to be able to design furniture that can reproduce itself.

Will carbon fibre gain ground in other areas?

Advances in manufacturing and processing are slowly cutting the cost of the material, and when carbon fibre becomes affordable, it will become more widely used. I think it will be able to replace aluminium and steel in product design, building construction, vehicle manufacturing and the aerospace industry.

In what ways can carbon fibre be regarded as one of the materials of the future?

Since we are beginning to understand the make-up of fibre-based materials on a molecular level, we can optimize their performance. The combination of scientific research and robotics has made it possible to optimize the way carbon fibre is handled, and how the fibres should be aligned and the strands interwoven. This knowledge has revealed that carbon fibre is something of a known quantity that can be researched and engineered especially for specific products, giving it a wider range of applications than many traditional materials.

Why did you decide to explore the future applications of paper?

Paper is a material with a wide range of uses besides the familiar ones. I use it in a new way in an attempt to highlight its qualities. Through this process I can create a chair that has a form and a degree of detailing that would not be possible to achieve in any other material. As a digital craftsman, I am interested in combining the digital and analogue worlds.

Bengtsson used layers of recycled paper to craft this strikingly sculptural chair. He says that inventing a method of using the material was 'a time-consuming but fascinating process. I used handmade techniques and digital craftsmanship to put thousands of sheets of paper together, take them apart and then put them back together again.' The chair that resulted is enormous, even though it is made from only thin sheets of paper without the need for a frame, joints or screws.

DYNAM
DESIGN

BIOMIMETIC DESIGN
EMPATHETIC OBJECTS
SYMBIOTIC DESIGNS
RAPID REPLICATION
FRACTAL FORMS
ROUGH LUXURY
FIBRE FURNITURE

Interviews with
MATHIEU LEHANNEUR
TOKUJIN YOSHIOKA
MORITZ WALDEMEYER

MIC
N

Shape-shifting materials, programmable surfaces, technological interfaces and labile components will transform everyday objects into interactive tools for dynamic lifestyles

Future worlds will be based on transition, and product design, in the same way as architecture and interiors, will reflect the ever-changing nature of the fast-paced lives we will lead. Products will be perceived as fluid rather than fixed, and technologized materials will enable designers to create forms that promote shifting relationships between user and object. As new paradigms of design unfold, the premise that a fixed structure should constitute the basis of design will be irrevocably reversed. Shape-shifting materials, programmable surfaces, technological interfaces and labile components will transform everyday objects into interactive tools for dynamic lifestyles.

The designs of the future will be created with transformable properties, and made dynamic and multifunctional as several different products are seamlessly combined into one. Dynamic designs will amplify the relationship between individuals and their surroundings, providing interactive shortcuts that make life more comfortable and information more accessible. Although most products will be controlled by a technical interface, no particular expertise or instruction manual will be needed to operate them. The designs of the future will be able to communicate with their user and sense his or her needs, subsequently providing interactive tutorials that explain how they should be used. As products begin to promote new types of interaction with their users, they will create symbiotic relationships that grow and evolve.

Although this degree of interactivity may seem to be light years away, it is already appearing over the horizon. Just as communications devices are being equipped with speaker-recognition software, voice-activated controls and interactive programs, ordinary domestic products are slowly becoming aligned with genetics, robotics, information technology and nanotechnology – a set of technologies known as GRIN. Such technologies are already beginning to shape the self-replicating products, empathetic objects, biomimetic designs and fractal forms that herald a new era in design. This unique moment in product design is truly cutting-edge, yet at the same time nothing new: for nearly a century, our lifestyles have been governed by principles of multifunctionality and the expectation that the practical problems of modern life will be solved by design. Future lifestyles portend more travel and less space, and interactive technology will underpin the multifunctional products that make it possible to get by with fewer objects.

The pervasiveness of the reductive approach to product design may mean that the early years of the twenty-first century will come to be known as the 'end of objects'. Not only will we live with fewer items, but also the integration of technology and product design will transform previously inert objects, effectively turning them into machines. And while future designs may operate with machine-like efficiency, they will have uniquely personal characteristics. Impersonal objects will become a thing of the past, as products are designed to promote empathy between object and user. Although many products will continue to be mass-produced, mass-customization processes will put an end to the manufacture of the 'cloned' products to which we are accustomed today.

The remainder of this chapter focuses on some of the leading developments within product design, highlighting many of the groundbreaking

OPPOSITE
Tokujin Yoshioka is one of the most prolific designers working in Japan today. His Invisibles collection for Kartell was developed to explore the use of clear acrylic in design. As well as creating an installation using transparent prism rods, shown here, Yoshioka designed furniture that took acrylic to new heights.

PAGE 128, TOP
This huggable atomic mushroom is the work of interactive design experts Anthony Dunne and Fiona Raby. Part of their Designs for Fragile Personalities in Anxious Times project, it offers a whimsical way of treating fears of nuclear annihilation.

PAGE 128, BOTTOM LEFT
Designed by Zaha Hadid for Established & Sons, the interlocking Nekton stools were created as a set of four.

PAGE 128, BOTTOM RIGHT
The Surface chair, created by British designers Terence Woodgate and John Barnard for Established & Sons, heralds a new direction for designs that combine structure and surface in a single expression.

PAGE 129
The Gaudi chair and stool by Amsterdam-based design studio Freedom Of Creation were inspired by the buildings and methodology of Spanish architect Antoni Gaudi. In addition, the designers used a computer program to calculate the chair's structure and shape.

ideas that herald the products of the future. Divided into seven sections, it investigates the dynamic exchanges taking place between product design and other disciplines, and reveals how science, technology and materials innovation are taking aesthetics dramatically forward. The chapter concludes with interviews with Mathieu Lehanneur, Tokujin Yoshioka and Moritz Waldemeyer, who reveal that a new generation of design is already beginning to reshape the world around us, signalling the way ahead.

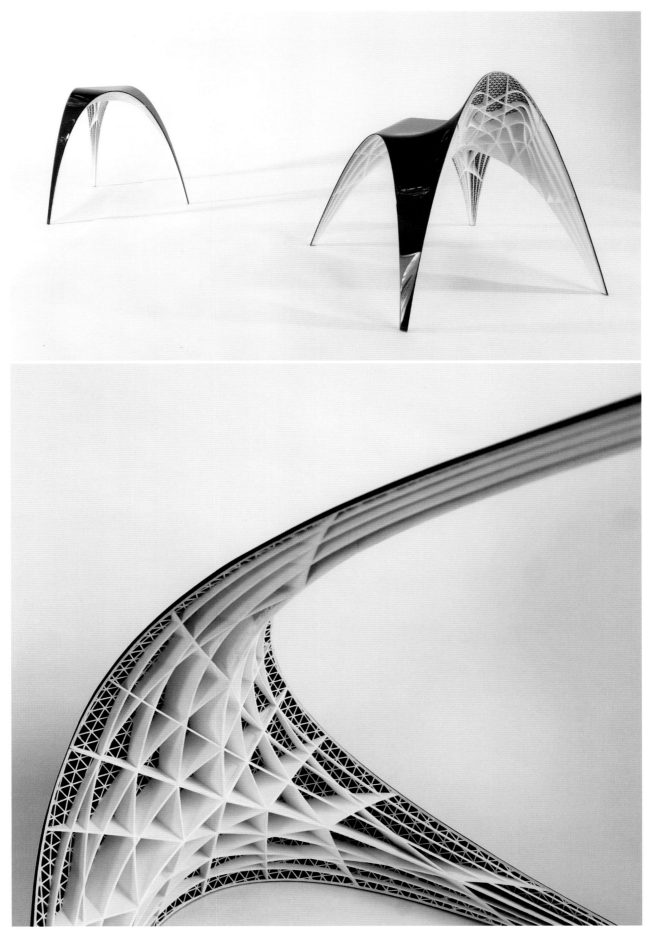

BIOMIMETIC DESIGN

New paradigms of sustainable design have led to a wider appreciation of organic materials and natural processes. The drive to re-create what nature does naturally has inspired designers to explore the science of biomimicry and, occasionally, to team up with scientists to create products that are hybrids of science and design.

Nature's know-how may be the result of millions of years of evolution, but technology provides short cuts that make it possible to imitate some of nature's forms in design. Researchers at the University of Reading's Centre for Biomimetics used advanced fibre technology to replicate the action of a pine cone's scales in a hi-tech, responsive textile. The researchers discovered that the scales – which open so that the pine cone can release its seeds – move in relation to changes in relative humidity, opening when it is dry and closing when it is wet. In particular, they found that, as the pine cone begins to dry out in relatively dry conditions, the layers that make up each of its scales release moisture at different rates, causing the scales to bend and flex. The researchers engineered the fibres in their textile to work in the opposite way. When they detect perspiration, the fibres curl open to ventilate the wearer; when the wearer's skin stops perspiring, the fibres dry out and close up, forming a smooth surface again.

Attempts to replicate in ceramic form the shatterproof shell of the abalone, a type of sea snail, indicate that nature's example may hold the key to producing self-replicating designs. Angela Belcher, a specialist in materials science and bioengineering at the Massachusetts Institute of Technology, discovered that the abalone forms its shell with the aid of certain proteins that bind

Mathieu Lehanneur's Local River concept consists of aquariums in which freshwater fish can be kept for food and glass domes for growing vegetables. The plants help to purify the water by extracting nitrates and other minerals.

The Bucky Ball seat by Mathieu Lehanneur resembles a geodesic dome, the structure made popular by American engineer and futurist Buckminster 'Bucky' Fuller. Upholstered in soft leather, the design provides supple, beanbag-style seating. Here, the seat is shown atop an indoor garden designed to help purify the air.

themselves to the calcium present in the ocean. In order to mimic this process, Belcher found a bacteriophage (a bacteria-infecting virus) with similar protein-binding abilities. She then introduced the bacteriophage to a form made from nanowires derived from semi-conductive materials. As it reproduced, the bacteriophage followed the shape created by the nanowires. Belcher is continuing to develop ways of combining hi-tech materials with self-replicating organisms. Her research is creating a blueprint for structures that will replicate themselves by 'growing' a pre-programmed shape.

Motorola's designers mined the ocean's depths to investigate the structures of crustacean shells. The result of their research was a remarkably durable cover for their i560 telephone. The cover is based on the tough outer shell of a lobster, which is composed of alternate layers of hard chitin and soft calcium carbonate. Similarly, the telephone's cover is constructed from alternate layers of rigid polycarbonate and flexible Santoprene, a rubber-like plastic. As a result, the i560 is one of the most durable mobile phones currently available, even meeting military standards for withstanding impact, vibration and extremes of temperature.

In their attempts to give surfaces that come into contact with water a hydrodynamic advantage, designers and scientists have been investigating how fish skin is formed. Despite having a skin rough enough to be used as sandpaper when dry, sharks slip through water with very little resistance. Scientists discovered that the fish's skin is covered in small, V-shaped protrusions made from the same material as its teeth. The rough surface actually reduces drag because the protrusions efficiently

channel water away from the shark's skin. Replicated on such sub-aquatic forms as propellers and boat hulls, shark skin-like systems of ridges and grooves cause water to spiral in microscopic vortices, drastically reducing drag. As a result, future marine vehicles will produce less drag and have more efficient propulsion, enabling them to consume less fuel.

EMPATHETIC OBJECTS

As the twenty-first century dawned, such devices as computers and mobile phones connected individuals to internet forums, virtual worlds and online social networks, creating relationships based on electronic stimuli rather than physical presence. Today, a new generation of interactive products is being designed to simulate certain types of social interaction, paving the way for future devices that will provide their users with a source of comfort and companionship.

Feelings of loneliness and social isolation were common causes of anxiety at the end of the twentieth century, and pets became a popular means of providing companionship for those who felt alone. Animals arouse soothing emotions, and for many people caged birds are an especially comforting source of beauty and entertainment. With that in mind, Miami-based artist Troy Abbott has created life-size 'video birds' with the appearance and mannerisms of adult rainbow finches. The birds appear on screens mounted inside a variety of real cages, singing and fluttering their wings from a virtual perch – all at the flip of a switch. Their owners can enjoy the companionship

BELOW, LEFT
The creation of American designer Noam Toran, Accessories for Lonely Men is a collection of conceptual objects intended to mimic the presence of a lover. When a cigarette is placed in the small hole of the 'Shared Cigarette' device, it 'inhales' the smoke and 'exhales' it through the vent below.

BELOW
The rotating metal bar of the 'Chest Hair Curler' is designed to mimic a finger playfully twirling strands of chest hair.

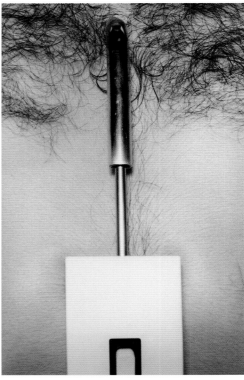

BELOW
This device simulates breathing, emitting subtle gusts of air to give the impression of the presence of a sleeping companion.

of a real bird without the obligation to clean its cage or feed it.

Noam Toran, an American designer based in London, has created a collection of one-off objects to alleviate loneliness, but his designs are intended to re-create a former lover rather than a loyal pet. Each design in the collection, titled Accessories for Lonely Men, is made to alleviate the loneliness that results from splitting up with a partner. The objects are organized with the evocativeness of an art installation, and are intended to produce some of the physical stimuli that a partner once provided.

The 'Sheet Stealer', for example, is a winding device that pulls the bedclothes towards the other side of the bed while the user is asleep. Another device is placed at the foot of the bed, where it allows the user to re-create the sensation of having a pair of cold feet pressed against his own. The 'Chest Hair Curler', a device with a rotating metal 'finger', is placed on the user's chest to simulate the feeling of having his chest hair gently stroked. The 'Shared Cigarette' is a smoking device intended to be activated after a solitary sex act. The device consists of two holes, one that holds and 'smokes' the

TOP
Bel-Air, Mathieu Lehanneur's air-filtering device, uses living plants to filter the air and boost its quality. Lehanneur promotes the use of plants that absorb airborne toxins, thereby improving the quality of the air.

BOTTOM
The K device by Lehanneur uses sheathed optical fibres, photoelectric cells, high-luminosity white LEDs and sensors to receive light, recharge itself and emit light when illumination levels fall.

OPPOSITE, TOP
Lehanneur's self-propelling dB device moves in the direction of high-decibel noises and counters them by emitting white noise. The device is intended to soften ambient sound.

OPPOSITE, BOTTOM
Lehanneur's C device automatically radiates heat when it senses a drop in temperature. The mobile device moves to where the temperature has fallen and stays there until the desired temperature has been reached.

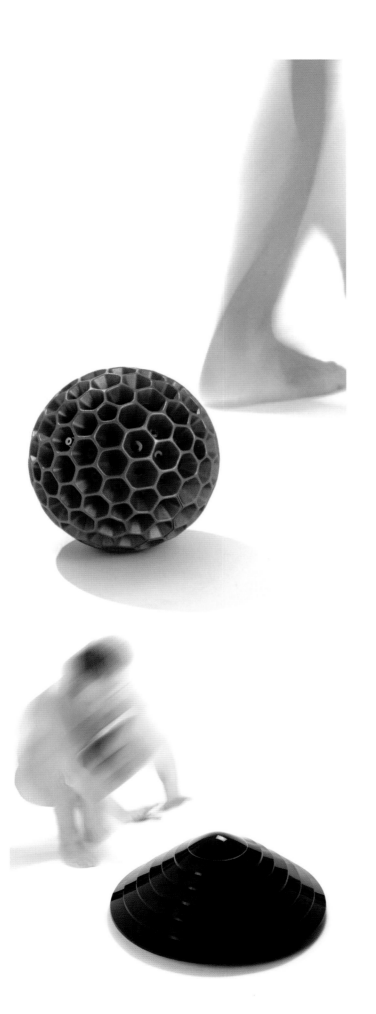

cigarette, and another that exhales smoke, allowing the user to re-create the act of sharing a cigarette with his lover.

Mathieu Lehanneur has taken a different approach to empathetic design, producing a series of four sensory, interactive designs that appear to anticipate their user's needs. The designs react to changes in temperature, ambient sound, light intensity and air quality by taking steps to bring them back to optimum levels. The C (for 'Celsius') device, which consists of heat sensors, infrared heat emitters and memory-shape alloys encased in an inverted cone of tiered elastomer bands, radiates heat when it senses a drop in temperature. The device automatically moves towards an area where the temperature has fallen, and remains there until the temperature rises. The K (for 'kelvin') device is a small, dodecahedron-shaped object covered with optical fibres that emit beams of light when illumination levels drop, providing an extra source of light for those suffering from light deprivation. O (for 'oxygen'), the third device in the series, is a transparent vessel filled with *Spirulina platensis*, which produces oxygen through photosynthesis when the device detects a rise in pollution levels. The last object in the series is the dB (for 'decibel') device, a ball that propels itself in the direction of high-decibel noises to counteract them by emitting white noise.

SYMBIOTIC DESIGNS

Symbiosis occurs when different life forms come together and establish relationships beneficial to both. In the future, a similar process will unfold between products and the people who use them, as designs equipped with technological interfaces gain the ability to follow their users' actions and sense changes in their surroundings. Rather than being strictly controlled by software, symbiotic designs will react in response to self-regulated systems, and acclimatize to changes around them. Some symbiotic products will be similar to the robotic pets designed to behave like a sentient being, making them seem more animal than mechanical. Such objects may even appear to have a life of their own, and many will be a normal part of everyday experience.

Today, intelligent objects are able to recognize their users through logins, identification codes and voice-recognition software. In the future, products may be activated by personal sensors, such as wearable radio-frequency identification tags or chip-like implants that identify the user and transmit his or her preferences. The exchanges between user and object will be mutually beneficial. Each time they are used, symbiotic designs will automatically connect to remote systems to update their software, just as many contemporary wireless devices do. The symbiotic devices will also glean data from their users' behaviour and the environment around them, while artificial intelligence will enable the devices to understand that the acquisition of information is necessary to heighten their usefulness and prolong their life spans. The designs of the future will adapt to technological trends much faster than those we use today, and will be made to last much longer.

Human interaction, already a standard activation prompt for a wide range of products, is the first step in engaging with a symbiotic design. The Clone Chaise chaise longue, by British designer Sam Buxton, activates itself when it detects a human presence. Its surface features a printed electroluminescent display unit that can react to its user and communicate information. As the user engages with the chaise longue, graphic representations of the heart and lungs begin to beat and breathe, as if bringing the chaise longue to life. The design is an evocative example of how exchanges between product and user can have an impact on both.

The London-based interactive design experts Anthony Dunne and Fiona Raby predict that robots will play a significant role in future lifestyles. Although most research in the area of artificial intelligence revolves around designing and programming robots to carry out specific tasks, Dunne and Raby have developed a series of prototype robots programmed to behave and react in ways that mirror human personality traits. For example, rather than programming surveillance robots with security technology, Dunne and Raby propose programming them with subroutines consistent with a human's experience of paranoia. The robots would behave as if they were suspicious, and appear to believe that most actions they observe could lead to security breaches. Another prototype has been fitted with retinal-scanning technology that enables it to identify the humans it 'knows', and intimidate those who avoid making eye contact.

Future generations of appliances will be interactive. They will be designed to respond to each

RIGHT
To investigate the future
relationship between humans
and robots, Anthony Dunne
and Fiona Raby developed a
series of prototype robots with
different functions and human
characteristics. The Sentinel
robot (top) is equipped with
retinal-scanning technology
to control who accesses our
private information. The
Needy One robot (bottom)
is programmed to behave like
a pet, relying on its user to
provide for its 'needs'.

PAGES 140–41
The Clone Chaise chaise longue
designed by Sam Buxton
features an electroluminescent
display unit that activates
when it detects a human
presence. As the user interacts
with the chaise longue, it
displays human vital signs
on its surface.

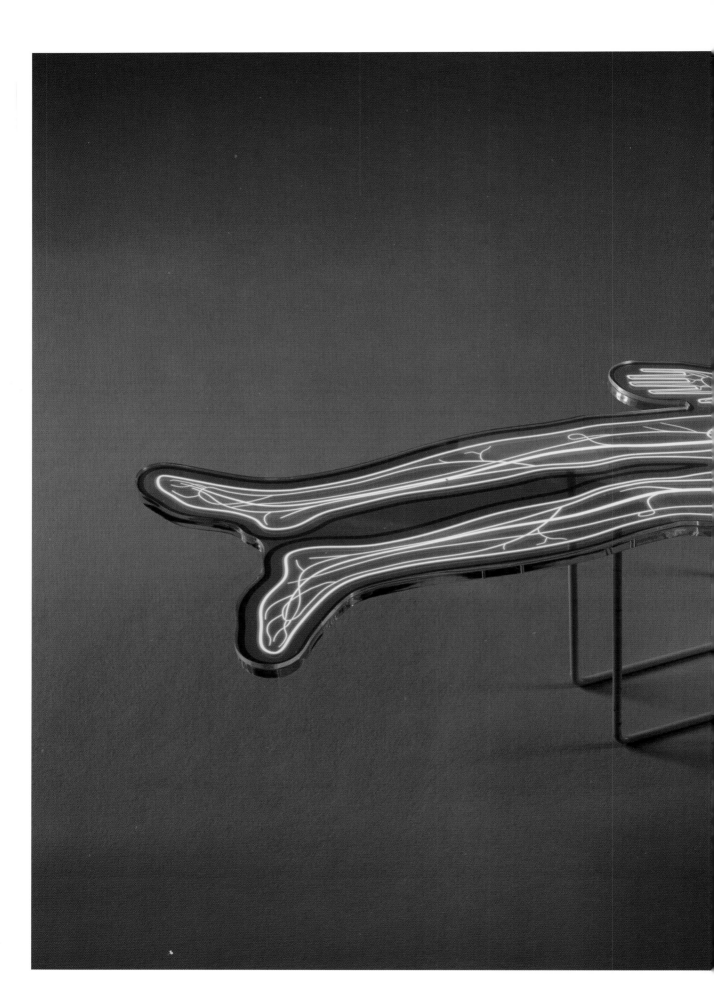

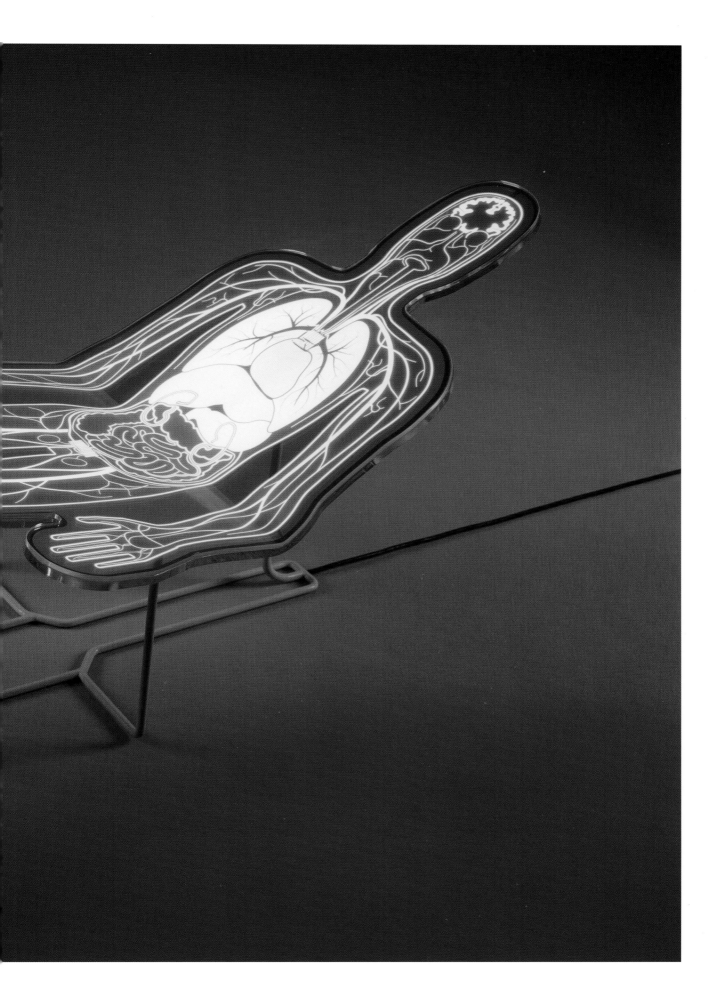

user individually, and orchestrate food, beverages and domestic needs according to individual requirements. London-based designer Onkar Kular has created a toaster that remembers the degree to which individual users like their bread to be toasted. Kular's Precision Toaster enables each member of a household to program the toaster with his or her preferred toasting time; once the toaster has identified the user, it automatically toasts the bread according to his or her specifications. By acquiring data about each member of the household, the toaster extends its usefulness to the users and, as a result, its length of active service.

Not all symbiotic designs will rely on human interaction. Products, appliances and interior surfaces will also respond to environmental factors, such as traffic, temperature, weather conditions and seasonal changes. London-based research studio Loop.pH is developing a decorative, light-emitting wallpaper that reacts to ambient noise levels. As sound levels increase, the wallpaper glows more brightly, creating dynamic links between interior surfaces and the space around them. Sensors embedded in the wallpaper transform it into a sensory device that is inextricably linked to environmental factors. The impact of the wallpaper on the space around it has yet to be measured, but changes in light levels are likely to effect human interaction, which, in turn, will affect the acoustics.

Simon Heijdens, a Dutch designer based in London, is known for his pioneering work with interactive surfaces. Lightweeds and Tree, two of Heijdens's digital installations, use projectors to cover walls with plant-inspired motifs, thus imbuing a room or a façade with naturalistic elements. The installations are linked to outdoor sensors activated by wind, sunshine and rain, which cause the wall motifs seemingly to blow in the wind, bend in the rain, rotate to follow the movement of the sun or shed leaves when autumn approaches. Heijdens's work breaks away from the predictability of static surfaces by aligning them with such unpredictable phenomena as the weather. Theories of climate change claim that human activity can directly affect the weather, suggesting a symbiotic relationship between mankind and the elements. Heijdens's work introduces design into the debate, proposing another relationship between man-made activity and natural forces.

RAPID REPLICATION

In the hi-tech design economy of the future, many products will be sold as CAD (computer-aided design) files rather than made in a factory or workshop. Replicating machines will be a basic feature of offices and homes, enabling individuals to download product files from commercial websites and produce the products locally. Such rapid-manufacturing devices as 3D printers and nano-assemblers will make it possible for individuals not only to manufacture products themselves but also to customize and adapt an original design to suit their own needs better.

A form of additive manufacturing technology known as 3D printing promises to revolutionize the way in which consumers acquire products. More user-friendly than similar technologies, 3D printing produces three-dimensional objects by building up successive layers of material. It was originally used by designers to create product prototypes, and is sometimes referred to as stereolithography or rapid prototyping. The technology uses an inkjet printing system that sprays layers of a semi-crystalline carbohydrate powder and liquid adhesive that harden as they come into contact with the air. With 3D printers, it is possible to produce objects in a single process, even those made of different materials or designed with mechanical properties. The RepRap desktop 3D printer, for example, one of the first to be made for home use, is capable of replicating such plastic objects as household accessories, decorative objects, jewellery and toys. As the technology becomes more advanced, it will be possible to produce such robust objects as tools and automotive parts. The RepRap machine is itself made from replicated plastic parts, meaning that it can be regarded as

Freedom Of Creation uses 3D printing technologies to produce a wide variety of objects, such as the lightweight Monarch stools shown here. The stools are made in a set of five different sizes, enabling them to be stacked for easy storage.

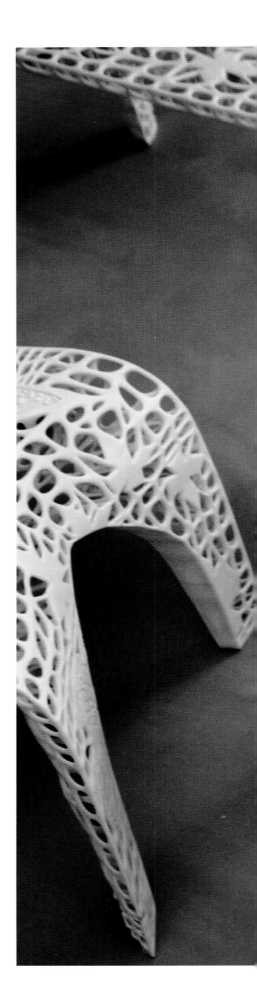

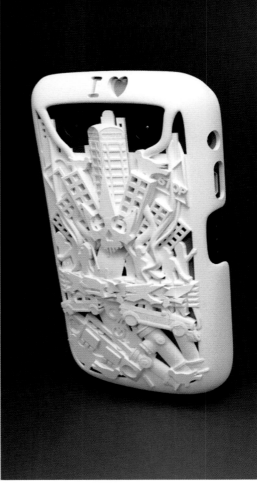

Freedom Of Creation is creating a new generation of objects that are both designed and manufactured digitally. The jewellery, footwear, mobile-phone cover and headphones shown here could eventually be downloaded over the internet and printed at home using a 3D printing machine. As more goods are manufactured by consumers at home, design companies will no longer need to maintain production infrastructures and manage stock quantities.

a self-replicating machine that can reproduce itself if programmed to do so.

A front-runner in the replicator revolution is Freedom Of Creation (FOC), an Amsterdam-based design studio pioneering rapid-manufacturing processes for a wide range of design applications. FOC designs products using such 3D modelling software applications as Solidworks and 3D Studio Max, and then fabricates the product using one of a number of 3D printing processes, including laser sintering and stereolithography. These processes enable FOC to create forms that would be impossible to produce using traditional moulding or pressing methods. Whether designed with a simple or a complex structure, a wide range of lighting, furniture and interior architectural fixtures can be produced by 3D printing. FOC was the first company to find fashion applications for the technology, producing chainmail-like non-woven textiles made up of interlocking pieces. It has created handbags, purses, watch straps and jewellery, and plans to produce sporting goods and footwear, too. An interview with FOC in the following chapter (page 194) provides a more detailed discussion of the company's working methods.

Future projections for the rapid manufacturing of objects include machines that can manipulate individual molecules to produce products, and mobile machines capable of replenishing their supply of base materials themselves. The nano-assembler, for example, will be able to create physical objects from computer files and inexpensive input materials. As it reads a product file, the machine will simultaneously assemble molecules or molecular fragments into the form required. A method based on 'swarm

intelligence' technology employs the complex self-organizing properties of 'swarms' of digital agents. The agents are molecules that have been manipulated to interact with one another in order to form specific objects. Other rapid-manufacturing methodologies promise to align design with artificial intelligence and genetic engineering, bringing product manufacturing into the realm of the latest scientific research and cutting-edge technology.

FRACTAL FORMS

As swarm intelligence, replicating machines and nanotechnology root design in the molecular level, furniture and lighting are beginning to acquire geometric shapes that mimic molecular structures. Molecules bond at angles that create triangular, octahedral and tetrahedral shapes, and form trigonal and pyramidal structures. These geometric forms are represented two-dimensionally in many of the 3D modelling and rendering programs used for furniture design, some of which include algorithmic modelling. The software scripts are able to create layered structures, fold flat planes and create unusual angles, making it possible to generate the fragmented shapes known as fractals. Many of the furniture designs that result have angular surfaces and bold, geometric silhouettes. Some pieces are made to interconnect and stack, be used as individual units of furniture or be linked modularly to create bigger pieces. Larger designs can also be used to create architectural structures that shape and define interior space.

One of the most visionary pieces of furniture to have emerged in recent years is the Starbrick unit, the result of a joint project between the Danish-Icelandic artist Olafur Eliasson and Zumtobel. Made in collaboration with Einar Thorsteinn, an architect and geometry expert, Starbrick is based on the idea of creating a space-defining modular unit that can either function as an individual light source or be combined with other units to create a larger design. Each unit consists of fractal planes joined at a variety of angles to form a star-like shape. Groups of units can be combined to create conventional linear forms or more complex geometric configurations that resemble molecular structures. The units can also form spirals, mimicking the dynamic coils of DNA helices.

The Starbrick's versatility is one of its key features. It can be attached to the ceiling or mounted on walls to provide a light fixture, while groups of Starbricks can be used as building blocks to form a wall of light or a dramatic ceiling. Starbricks can also be stacked into columns or interlinked to create an interior grotto. Since the Starbrick blurs the boundaries between individual pieces of furniture and interior architecture, it represents a new direction for design.

Fractal forms often feature in the work of Julian Mayor, a British designer known for his forward-thinking designs. Mayor uses 3D computer modelling to create complex pieces of furniture and whole environments. His surfaces are characterized by dynamic folds and extreme angles, which seem to warp the geometry of space. Mayor's General Dynamic armchair, one of his limited-edition designs, is distinguished by origami-like folds that generate fractal shapes throughout the chair's structure and surface. The shapes resemble the facets of cut gemstones, giving the lacquered fibreglass chair a strikingly sculptural appearance.

Mayor based his *Regency* series of outdoor sculptures on fractal planes so that their surfaces would appear to be in a state of flux, giving them a dynamic seldom seen in a static object. The angles and folds in the sculptures' metal surfaces create an unexpected play of light and shadow, as though the sculptures were pulsating in the changing light. Mayor's sculpture *Frame*, also made of metal, is another of his works based on fractal shapes. Unlike Mayor's other pieces, however, the sculpture has no surface, enabling its structural supports to remain

The Starbrick, developed by artist Olafur Eliasson in collaboration with Zumtobel and Einar Thorsteinn, is a fractal-like modular unit that can function as an individual light source or be combined with others to produce large-scale designs. The units can be suspended from the ceiling as pendant lamps or be built up vertically in tiers to create lighting installations.

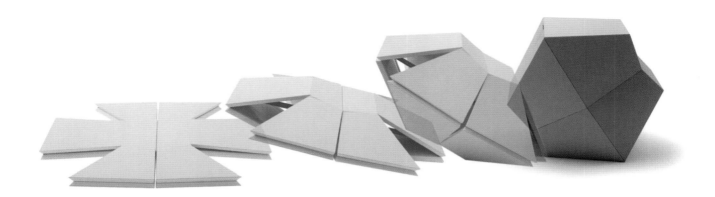

visible. *Frame*'s stark geometric outline brings to mind three-dimensional renderings of molecular modelling, as if representing a structure that could be expanded infinitely on larger scales.

Belgian designer Maarten De Ceulaer's modular lighting system, made to resemble a molecular model, is designed to expand exponentially as more illumination is required. Known as the Nomad Light Molecule, the system consists of small, interconnected spheres of light that can be detached to provide individual light-sources. When fully charged, a single detached sphere will emit light for approximately four hours; after that time, it can be reattached to the system to be recharged. The system is completely amorphous: the lamps can be attached to any part of it, and at every conceivable angle, enabling it to be configured in a range of diverse shapes.

True to its name, the striking Fractal.MGX table created by German design duo Gernot Oberfell and Jan Wertel was inspired by the fractal growth patterns of the stems and branches of plants and trees. The designers used mathematical calculations to simulate a tree's growth, resulting in a design composed of tree-like forms that 'grow' upwards from the floor and divide into clusters of branches that merge to form a solid tabletop. The table is made from epoxy resin and produced by stereolithography. Despite the table's complex shape, the stereolithographic process enabled it to be manufactured as a single piece, without any seams or joins. The design methodology behind the table aligns the randomness of nature with the precision of geometry, creating a visionary example of how the two can be combined.

Those spending the night in the R.E.M. bed created by Italian designers Riccardo Blumer and Matteo Borghi will be sleeping in comfort and style. Blumer and Borghi's design consists of a metal structure that has been angled into a range of fractal shapes and covered in an elastic fabric, which gives the structure a sleek surface and a sense of volume. Although the fractal shapes are not uniform, the straight edges that join them lend the bed a polyhedron-like silhouette. The randomness of the fractals' shapes breaks away from strict linear geometry, softening and subduing the overall shape.

Functional and efficient, the Meister Eder seat is a flexible, lightweight fractal design created by the Berlin-based duo of Nina Farsen and Isabel Schöllhammer. Completely flat when not in use, Meister Eder forms a striking sixteen-sided geometric seat when a hidden rubber band is released. The efficiency of flat-pack furniture has become a hallmark of contemporary design, and the ease with which Meister Eder can be assembled indicates that such furniture is likely to continue long into the future.

ABOVE
The Meister Eder seat was designed by Nina Farsen and Isabel Schöllhammer. It can be folded completely flat, and then transformed into a sixteen-sided seat by releasing a hidden rubber band.

OPPOSITE, TOP LEFT
Turkish designer Serhan Gurkan's Love design can be used as either a stool or a table. The modular nature of the design means that several can be combined to form a bench or a seating cluster.

OPPOSITE, TOP RIGHT
Gurkan's Gazelle design is produced in a range of heights, enabling it to be used as a bar surface, a side table or a high stool.

OPPOSITE, BOTTOM
The geometric Kubo table by Danish designer Rasmus Fenhann is based on a cuboctahedron, a polyhedron with twenty-four edges of the same length. Because this particular shape is one of the strongest polyhedra, the table is structurally sound despite its light weight and spare use of materials.

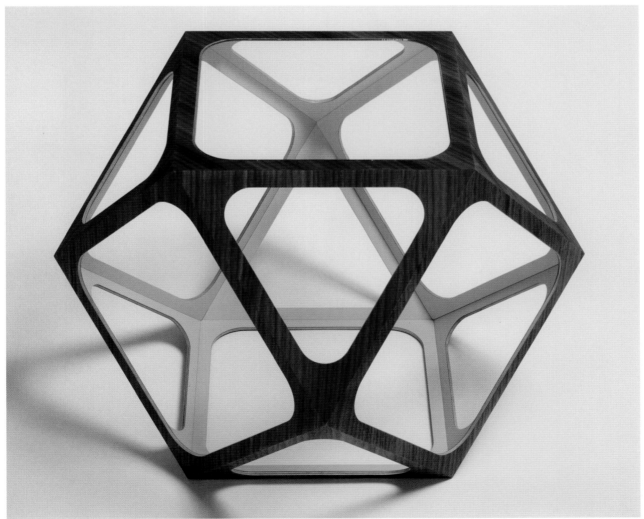

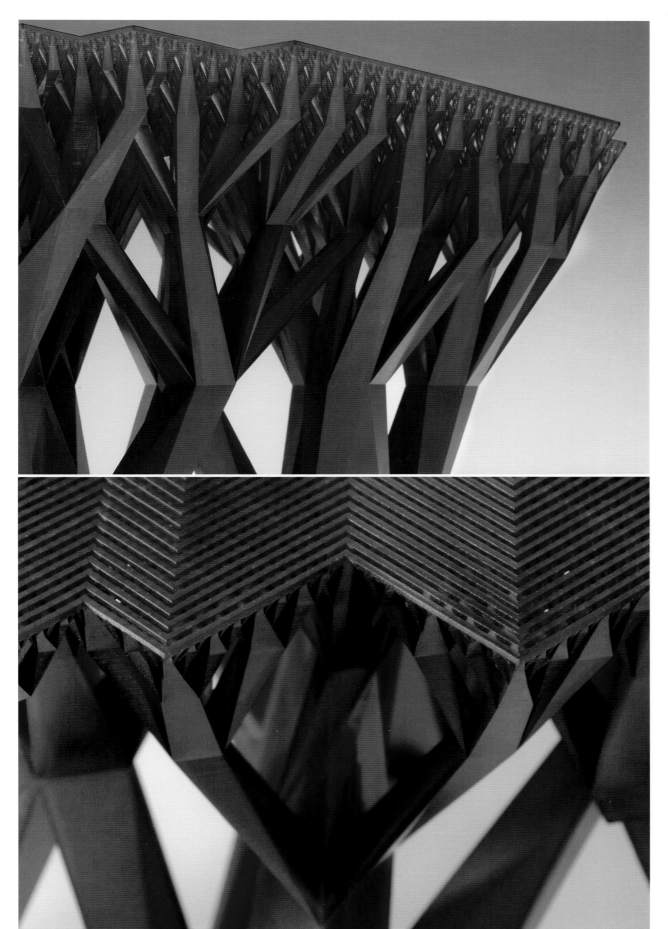

ROUGH LUXURY

Refined but rough-hewn shapes cut out of dense materials are aligning craft traditions with luxury design. This chair by Simon Heijdens was chiselled out of marble using traditional techniques and contemporary know-how, revealing that time-honoured craftsmanship can play a significant role within design, both today and in the future.

As though rising in opposition to rapid manufacturing, computer-aided design and strict geometric silhouettes, craft practices are becoming increasingly popular among contemporary designers, and promise to be a central part of product design in the decades to come. The preservation of craft skills and artisan production methods has led to the revival of some of the guilds established in medieval Europe. Much of the guilds' output was regarded as luxury goods; in the future, their time-honoured craft techniques will emerge as the hallmarks of luxury objects.

The interest in craft practices and the appreciation of handmade objects are dramatically changing industrial design. With craft skills come such materials as wood, natural fibres, clay, metal and glass. Whether in the form of gleaming metalware, delicate ceramics or sleek wooden objects, handmade items have a unique patina that is more appealing than the uniform surfaces of mass-produced objects. Handmade goods have become so popular in recent years that manufacturers are introducing flexible computer-aided manufacturing systems capable of giving mass-produced items a customized finish. Popularly known as 'mass customization', these systems combine the low unit costs of mass production with the trademark individuality of a handmade object.

Customization is regarded as a future frontier in design, motivating designers to become more directly involved in the fabrication process from the earliest stages of design. The use of natural materials and traditional techniques is resurfacing as a key theme in design education, which is coupling it with CAD programs that update craft practices for a new generation of design. When it comes to marrying craft techniques to industrial design, British designer Simon Hasan is a leader in his field, creating products that bridge the gap between mass production and handcraftsmanship. In particular, Hasan is reviving the ancient woodland craft of wood cleaving, which he combines with modern TIG-welded carbon steel, stoneware and leather to create collections of vernacular furniture. Rather than use a saw, Hasan splits locally sourced oak along the grain. This technique does not divide the wood uniformly, but creates uniquely shaped pieces of wood defined by the density of the grain. Hasan then uses the wooden pieces as, for example, legs for a stool, combining them with a seat shaped by a modern machine. Hasan's working methods combine an ancient craft practice with contemporary manufacturing, resulting in a unique object every time.

London-based designer Max Lamb creates contemporary furniture using basic craft skills, and makes instructive videos that show the consumer how to fabricate his designs. Lamb's Hexagonal Pewter Stool is made using a simple sand-casting technique that can be performed in the garden or on a beach. Pewter is heated until molten, then poured into a mould sculpted directly out of a patch of sand. Once the metal cools, the sand is dug away to reveal a pewter stool. Lamb's Poly Chair, also designed to be made by the consumer, appropriates the tools and techniques used for wood carving and applies them to a rigid block of polyurethane. As the soft material is cut away, the seat, back and sides of the chair are formed and sculpted into contours. Approximately half an hour is needed to carve the chair, and a further ten minutes to coat it with a rubbery finish. Lamb's designs encourage consumers to take a hands-on approach to the goods they acquire, honing and practising time-honoured craft techniques as they do so. His videos, meanwhile, enable him to communicate directly with consumers, while also enabling them to share authorship of the finished product.

In a move to express himself as an artist, Israeli designer Arik Levy created a body of work that explored the complex relationship between the natural and the man-made. The collection included Levy's polygonal sculpture *Rock*, which transformed a boulder into a sleek table. The collection was intended to blur the boundaries between art and design, yet also erase the distinctions between the rough textures found in the natural world and the smooth shapes characteristic of design.

OPPOSITE, TOP
Simon Hasan's furniture
is inspired by British craft
traditions. Hasan's use
of split timber and leather
craftsmanship came
together in this rustic yet
contemporary-looking stool.

OPPOSITE, BOTTOM
The rigid leather of Hasan's
handmade Twist bench was
formed using the traditional
processes of boiling, stretching
and tanning. Although the
bench is regarded as a luxury
item, the tough leather is
intentionally far removed from
the soft textures usually
associated with high-quality
leather furniture.

TOP
Hasan's side tables combine
the medieval leather-working
technique of cuir bouilli with
contemporary brass surfaces
polished to a high sheen.

BOTTOM
This steel-and-leather
credenza by Hasan consists
of a carbon-steel carcass part-
covered by a hand-stitched,
moulded leather shell. Brass
fittings and thick leather
handles accentuate the rustic
robustness of the design.

FIBRE FURNITURE

Technological breakthroughs are making fibre research one of the most exciting sources of innovation within contemporary design. Fibres are moving far beyond their associations with fashion and soft furnishings, and are being used to create uniquely textured objects with unprecedented strength and flexibility. A wide variety of fibres are being seamlessly integrated with technology, and fibre research has emerged as an interdisciplinary area linking science with such commercial realms as furniture, vehicle design and medicine.

Today, furniture designers are beginning to use fibres that allow them to produce the seat, frame and surface of a chair as a single object. Some designers are exploring the potential of memory materials, carbon filaments and ultra-strong synthetic aramid fibres, even using such techniques as weaving, crocheting, braiding and felting to craft tables and chairs. By finding applications for new fibres and pushing the boundaries of traditional ones, designers are opening up exciting possibilities for furniture design.

After reading an article about new developments in textile technology, Japanese designer Tokujin Yoshioka decided to explore the potential that fibres hold for product design. Yoshioka discovered that fibres perform well when subjected to force, by absorbing energy and dispersing it throughout their structure. Yoshioka's research led him to polyester elastomer fibres, which can be moulded into new shapes using heat. Yoshioka compressed several kilograms of the fibres into the shape of a half cylinder. Next, pressure was used to 'sculpt' the half cylinder into a chair, which was then bound in a fireproof membrane and packed inside a cardboard tube.

Finally, the chair – still inside the tube – was heated in a kiln at 104°C (219°F) until the fibres had fused together, enabling them to hold their shape even after the chair had been removed from the cardboard tube.

The design that resulted is known as the Pane Chair (in reference to the baking of bread, or *pane* in Italian), one of the first chairs to be completely formed by a heat process. Yoshioka's method of using pressure and energy to create a solid shape mimics a felting technique, but it bonds the fibres through the application of heat rather than friction. Yoshioka later used the principles behind the Pane Chair to design seating for Italian manufacturer Moroso, creating the Panna Chair. This more recent design consists of polyurethane foam attached to a metal skeleton and textured upholstery woven from thick yarns. Stitching in the upholstery helps to reinforce the chair's shape: an unbroken, continuous seam connects the base, back and sides, while other seams anchor the armrests in place.

Yoshioka has also used fibres as the basis for a chair that does not contain a single textile substrate. The Venus chair was constructed using naturally forming crystals. First, Yoshioka grouped bundles of fibres together to create a basic chair shape, complete with arms, legs, seat and backrest. The chair form was then immersed in a special liquid, and over time crystals began to grow around the fibres, expanding exponentially to form a dense, rock-like material. Once the liquid had been drained away, an assemblage of crystals in the shape of a chair came into view, but not a single fibre could be seen. The Venus chair demonstrates how tiny fibres can be used to create solid forms of considerable strength and weight.

Designed by Bertjan Pot for the Audax Textile Museum in The Netherlands, the Big String Sofa was created to divide the museum's entrance from the cafe. The high-backed seat was crafted from polypropylene string arranged in a rainbow of bright colours.

Award-winning Dutch designer Marcel Wanders was one of the first European designers to explore the use of fibres in the manufacture of furniture. Made for the Dry Tech series produced by Droog Design, Knotted Chair is a lightweight lounger fabricated from aramid fibres. Using a macramé technique, Wanders knotted several hundred metres of aramid around a carbon-fibre core to form a chair. The chair was then impregnated with epoxy resin and hung in a frame to dry. The fibres hardened as they dried, creating a durable, lightweight structure that is both flexible and strong. The Crochet Chair, another successful design, is also made from fibres. Every part of the armchair was crocheted, making it a *tour de force* in the use of traditional techniques and tactile fibres. Wanders used impregnation processes to rigidify the fibres, enabling the chair to hold its shape when used.

In collaboration with fellow Dutch designer Bertjan Pot, Wanders co-designed the lightweight Carbon Chair. The chair was fabricated completely by hand, using carbon fibre as the only structural material. Carbon-fibre rope was coiled to form the seat, backrest, rims and legs, then coated with epoxy resin to prevent the fibres from uncoiling. Although the chair's mesh-like pattern appears to be random, it was carefully calculated to maximize the strength of the carbon fibre. For example, each of the strands of carbon-fibre rope that make up the seat and backrest connects with one of the four bolts used to attach the legs. Despite its strength, carbon fibre is surprisingly lightweight, making the furniture crafted from it cost-effective to ship. Paradoxically, carbon-fibre furniture may actually reduce carbon emissions, placing it in the realm of sustainable design.

RIGHT
Tokujin Yoshioka used fibres as the basis for his Venus chair. Bundles of fibres were grouped into a chair shape, then immersed in liquid (top). Over time, crystalline structures formed around the fibres, and slowly expanded to create a rock-hard armchair (centre). Material samples (bottom) show how the fibres looked before they were immersed in the liquid, and how they were hidden from view after the crystals had formed.

OPPOSITE
Mathias Bengtsson creates his carbon-fibre furniture by stringing a series of filaments between two circular shapes. The fibres are then impregnated with an epoxy solution to enhance their durability and strength.

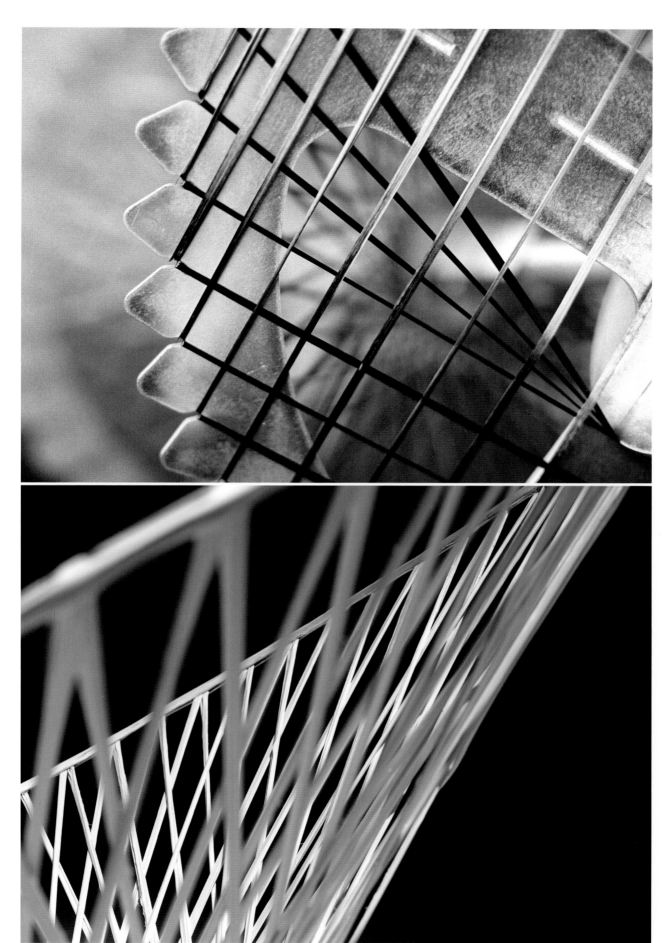

MATHIEU LEHANNEUR

Paris-based designer Mathieu Lehanneur has a vast repertoire. His creations range from sensory designs that interact with other objects to futuristic environments that soothe the human psyche. Lehanneur was one of the first designers successfully to combine organic materials with digital technology, resulting in designs that use live organisms to purify the air or equip built structures with living parts. His interior design projects include sleek hotel rooms equipped with hi-tech environmental controls, organic restaurants with living designs, luxury private offices, sleek fashion boutiques and even a strip club. Although these spaces are diverse in scope, each one bears the hallmarks of Lehanneur's signature conceptual approach. When asked to discuss the future of design in the following interview, Lehanneur thought long and hard before commenting in his characteristically cerebral style.

What inspired you to make empathetic designs?

Many factors, but take my dB product as an example [page 137]. I noticed how we, in our daily life, at home or at the office, are continuously disturbed by noise, and decided to see if I could alleviate this by creating a kind of sound buffer to filter out noise pollution without isolating people. Rather than designing earmuffs or earplugs, I just worked with the complexity of the human brain to come up with dB, which is a white-noise diffuser. White noise is the sum of all frequencies that are audible to the human ear, brought to the same intensity. The noise is like a 'shhhhhhhhhhhhh', and is the perfect and most neutral sound for our ears and our brain. When you hear white noise, your brain immediately focuses on it; you are not disturbed by other sounds any more. In order to make white noise a little bit active and reactive, I created a rolling ball. So dB is capable of identifying a noise, of rolling towards it, and of neutralizing it by emitting white noise.

Is there a market for empathetic design right now?

Absolutely! When my empathetic designs are displayed in exhibitions, trade fairs or stores, they always attract a crowd. Not just because they are novel, but also because everyone has an instinctive ability to understand them. Unlike many hi-tech products, their use does not have to be explained.

How will we live with design in the future?

Not as we live in our interiors today, which is similar to how prehistoric people were living in their caves. I say this because we do not interact with our house and our homes to help us to live better, because we just fill them with objects rather than designing the home to be interactive. In the future we should live in our interiors in a symbiotic way, just as we live in the skin and organs of our bodies. A fully reactive interior could monitor our body temperature, watch how our pupils dilate and glean information from our scent to adjust temperature, light and sound levels automatically and constantly adapt them to our needs. We have an advantage over the cavemen because we have the technology and materials to make it happen. It could even mimic a natural process, because new technologies, sensors and materials can help us work and play in an instinctive way. Look at the current developments in sensory scent technology – that is just one example.

How do you think future design can bring mankind closer to nature?

Think about how a baby matures inside its mother's womb. Everything is perfectly conceived to help it to grow, to be protected, to evolve step by step. The womb is the most adaptive and reactive interior we could ever imagine, and I think products and interiors could provide the same biological comfort. And when they are no longer needed, they could biodegrade just as organic forms do. Our body,

for example, is a form full of cells that disappear day after day. I believe that this process could also apply to objects and architecture, designing them with the ability to disappear by themselves.

Will science play a bigger role in design in the years ahead?

When I first started working as a designer, I found inspiration in astrophysics, biology and pharmaceutical research, so I contacted scientists, researchers and laboratories to find out more about them. At the time, the people I spoke to often thought it was odd that a designer was contacting them, but today, they often contact me and ask if we can collaborate. Scientists have understood that collaborations with designers can give them new directions; that we can help them use their research to create a product, and sometimes even help them build a business model around their research.

What kind of designs would you like to develop in the future?

I would like to develop some invisible designs. It is more realistic than you think, because the visible field is actually a very small part of our world. As human beings, we exist in the midst of invisible fields, such as brainwaves, radio frequencies, magnetic fields, energy *etc*. I think it is possible to harness such things and use them as a basis for future design.

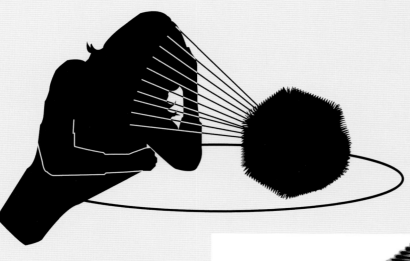

TOP
This is Lehanneur's sketch
for K, his light-generating
device intended to boost light
levels. K can also help those
suffering from seasonal
affective disorder (SAD).

CENTRE
For his *Age of the World*
exhibition at the Issey Miyake
boutique in Paris in 2009,
Lehanneur created a series of
enamelled ceramic containers.
The pieces were made to reflect
age distributions within the
populations of ten different
countries, among them France,
Egypt, Russia and the United
States. The piece shown here
represents Japan.

BOTTOM
The Bucky Ball seat moulds to
the body at every turn, shifting
into different shapes as the
user changes position.

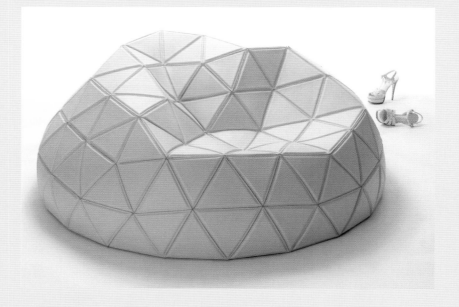

TOKUJIN YOSHIOKA

Japanese product designer Tokujin Yoshioka comes from a fashion background, having both studied under Issey Miyake and, from 1988 to 1992, worked for him. Since establishing his own design studio in 2000, however, Yoshioka has used such materials as organic crystal, glass and resin to create furniture, lighting and electronics. As well as producing products under his own name, Yoshioka has designed furniture for manufacturers in Japan and Europe. Although he is known as a designer of minimal forms, Yoshioka is primarily interested in creating forms that express such intangibles as feelings, concepts and the senses. He regards his work as being close to nature, and takes his inspiration from such naturalistic forms and elements as wind, water and light. When interviewed for this book, the designer drew on aspects of his own practice to make projections for the future of design generally.

What motivates you to create new forms?

It is the challenge of producing something that has never been achieved before. My process requires a lot of experimentation, not just to develop the idea itself but also to find ways to produce it. I try to design things that can touch human senses or emotions rather than just create an arrangement of forms. Creating something that is completely new also creates a new experience for the public, which I like, too.

If you were invited to design a space for the future, what would you create?

I would create a space that is related to senses, and not to forms. It is a space that will elicit all kinds of emotions, being full of surprise and delight. I think it would be great if new technology could contribute to the creation of such a space.

Do you think that using natural processes to produce products can create as many possibilities as technological processes do?

In recent years, such technological developments as computer graphics have enabled us to realize various complicated visions, but I have discovered that nature holds more new creative possibilities than we can imagine. I discovered this when I came up with the idea of designing the Venus chair [page 158], a chair grown from natural-crystal structures, because half of the design is created by me and the other half is created by natural phenomena.

How do you think the discipline of design will unfold in the future?

This is a time of big change in the definition of design, because all kinds of creative activities – art, design and architecture – are discussed in the same voice. The widespread use of the internet is a factor in sharing and circulating ideas among the creative disciplines. I hope that we can build a future based on the creations of our past.

Is product design already beginning to move in new directions?

Commodities are getting smaller and smaller through digitalization, so in the near future I believe that there will be an end to arranging forms, and that the act of experience will become the creation itself.

TOP
The window display created by Yoshioka for French luxury label Hermès features an image of a model who appears to be blowing 'life' into one of the company's classic scarves. The image is back-projected on to a screen set flush within the display surface. A steady stream of air blowing the scarf gives the impression that it is the model who is making it move.

BOTTOM
This photograph shows Yoshioka himself seated in one of the Invisible clear-acrylic chairs he designed for Kartell.

MORITZ WALDEMEYER

Moritz Waldemeyer is a German-born designer and engineer based in London. He has designed technological interfaces for such visionaries as Zaha Hadid, Marcel Wanders, Philippe Starck, Ron Arad and Hussein Chalayan, and has worked with many other leading architects and designers. Waldemeyer has pioneered the incorporation of micro-LEDs and laser lighting into such items as clothing and furniture. His collaboration with Chalayan, for example, for Chalayan's 'Airborne' Autumn/Winter 2007 collection, resulted in a dress that projects moving images across its surface. Waldemeyer's funky Disco Table features built-in laser lights, an iPhone/iPod dock and a haze machine. A leading expert on technological innovation and high-end design, Waldemeyer seems to be shaping the future as much as he is watching it unfold, as the following interview reveals.

What key movements will develop in product design in the future?

Desktop manufacturing methods will shift from being very expensive to being accessible to all. In particular, 3D printing is maturing as a technology, and together with other computer-based methods will make the path from idea to working prototype faster and more advanced. So, soon, we are going to see more sophisticated projects and even small production runs coming straight off the designer's desk. This movement will be paralleled by a trend to go back to nature and a re-evaluation of methods from the past in order to create a more sustainable and livable future. It will be interesting to see how these two opposite trends interact with each other; I think the mix of the two will be a new source of innovation.

In what ways are the materials and technologies you use shaping future aesthetics?

I don't think that future aesthetics will result directly from materials or technologies, but from the unusual combination of the two and the innovations that result. After all, such materials as Corian, organza, LEDs and circuit boards have been around for decades, yet very few attempts have been made to explore a combination of these materials. I really enjoy looking for inspiration in unlikely places and bringing ingredients into the design world that seem to be unrelated. For example, I combined the ancient Chinese art of wushu kung fu with fashion and electronics, and ended up creating some interesting objects as a result. The weapons, the LED uniforms and the amazing photographs and video footage sparked a few hi-tech innovations I made. For me, the future is in the destruction of boundaries, and this combination of tradition and innovation is a good example of that.

Are there any obstacles that should be addressed and overcome now in order to help design advance more rapidly?

My experience while teaching at the Royal College of Art in London indicates that young designers do not lack innovative ideas, but the technical knowledge to realize them. I did not receive a classic design education, and I have a feeling that my engineering background gives me an advantage. I think design education should be based on a strong technical foundation, on which the aesthetic and artistic side can be built later.

Can your work enable products to become intelligent, empathetic or symbiotic?

The quality that I am most interested in is giving objects charm – making them more human thanks to small doses of intelligence. So, for example, I managed to give this very cool and minimalist coffee table a second personality by turning it into a kinky go-go dancing cage at the flick of a switch. At night, its secret alter ego suddenly takes over, and people can relate to that.

TOP
Waldemeyer embedded hundreds of LEDs in jackets for the four members of the American rock band OK Go. The illuminating jackets were among the first technologized garments to be seen in menswear – and they almost stole the show.

BOTTOM
Waldemeyer takes his inspiration from a wide variety of sources. Shown here are some of the contemporary weapons he designed for the ancient Chinese martial art of wushu kung fu. Working with British wushu champion Steve Coleman, Waldemeyer created a show that combined martial-art manoeuvres with innovative lighting effects.

HYPER
CES

VIRTUAL HORIZONS
THE INVISIBLE
REACTIVE MEMBRANES
SWITCHABLE SURFACES
INTERACTIVE TECHNOLOGY

Interviews with
JANE HARRIS
FREEDOM OF CREATION

SURFA

In architecture and design, the recent trend of combining the structure and surface of an object in a single expression is erasing the distinctions between the two

The surface is a sensory realm, an expanse defined by sight, touch, shape and texture. Surfaces have long held a special significance for humans, and the tradition of embellishing the outermost layer of an object stretches back for millennia. Over time, cladding, colour, ornamentation and paint finishes have evolved as methods of concealing the mechanics of construction, or, conversely, as means of drawing attention to them.

In architecture and design, the recent trend of combining the structure and surface of an object in a single expression is erasing the distinctions between the two. The continuous, sinuous band of the Möbius strip, for example, has provided inspiration for fashion designers, and features strongly in the striking contours of the Design Museum Holon in Israel, created by Ron Arad. Architects and designers are also finding inspiration in the mathematical model of the Klein bottle, a form that has no identifiable inside or outside, translating its mathematically determined surfaces into three-dimensional objects. Designs based on such concepts break down the divisions between surface and structure. They challenge the notion of inner and outer, and redraw the boundaries of ordinary three-dimensional Euclidean space.

While the role of the surface is changing radically today, it promises to be even more dramatically different in the future. In addition to designers and architects, haptic scientists (those concerned with touch), software developers and computer-graphics specialists are also redefining the role of the surface in future lifestyles. The work of these practitioners is transforming conventional forms into responsive surfaces that can access information portals and virtual domains via integrated screens, keyboards and computer interfaces.

Although virtual domains may seem to be the stuff of science fiction, they are becoming a real part of everyday life. Satellite navigation, online maps, training simulations, computer games and other interactive software applications underpin actual experiences with virtual counterparts. The virtual and the physical are merging on the surfaces of screens, with graphic interfaces, computer-generated displays and touch-operated programs fusing real-time realities with fabricated environments. Virtual worlds will be easily accessed through an abundance of interactive surfaces, leading individuals to base their perception of their surroundings on what is happening on screen. Just as interactive technology is shaping our current lifestyles, virtual worlds will play an important role in how we interpret our surroundings in the future.

The remainder of this chapter is divided into five sections, and includes interviews with Jane Harris and Freedom Of Creation. In the first two sections, 'Virtual Horizons' and 'The Invisible', the innovations that connect surfaces to the virtual world or make them disappear altogether are described and discussed. Reactive and interactive technology promises to revolutionize the surfaces of the future, and some of the radical forms that are already beginning to emerge are outlined in the final three sections: 'Reactive Membranes', 'Switchable Surfaces' and 'Interactive Technology'.

This interactive surface offers a compelling new visual experience. Created by designer Kyota Takahashi and architect Akihisa Hirata for Canon's NeoReal installation exhibited at the Milano Salone of 2010, the surface reacts to the user by displaying spontaneous shapes and unexpected images that move and change colour.

Ron Arad's Design Museum Holon in Israel is characterized by a large scupltural feature based on the Möbius strip. The building's design combines structure and surface in a single expression, heralding a new direction for architectural surfaces.

VIRTUAL HORIZONS

A surface does not have to represent reality; it can be a space for fantasy and imagination. Real surfaces are used to display virtual environments, thereby incorporating illusion into our perception of reality. Such environments constitute a non-material aspect of experience that is nonetheless very real. The information and experiences afforded by virtual environments will reinvent the role and function of the surface, transforming it from a barrier into a gateway for wider experience.

The surfaces created using 3D animation software are digitally modelled and manipulated to produce mesh-like forms seemingly underpinned and supported by invisible digital skeletal structures. Known as 'rigging', the process is based on mathematical calculations that simulate the effects of gravity and the presence of shadow and light. Such software as Motion Capture and CG can be used to simulate fur, hair and skin, and such special effects as fire, water and clouds. The resulting virtual environments are often photorealistic, enabling virtual characters and objects to move and interact with one another in a manner that appears highly realistic to the viewer.

As virtual environments become a component of real life, they map out new directions for architecture and design. The virtual worlds created on the internet use graphic interfaces, online gaming tools and telecommunications technologies to facilitate community networks based on user-generated content. Second Life and Entropia Universe, for example, provide architects and designers with a forum in which to develop and promote new work in real time. Easy-to-use, built-in 3D modelling tools enable users to create an avatar, build virtual objects and simulate actual surfaces.

Several real-world companies, including Philips Design, have established a presence in Second Life, where their virtual members of staff are managed by their real-life counterparts. Peugeot, the French car manufacturer, has created an island in Second Life on which fans of automotive design can visit an exhibition hall, a conference room and an information area for the exchange of ideas. Avatars are invited to submit entries for annual design contests, in which Peugeot's Second Life equivalent awards the winners with cash prizes paid in Linden dollars (Second Life's virtual currency).

Virtual worlds represent open and free environments in which materials, style and functionality are not limited by budgetary constraints or practical concerns, and in which designs need not relate to objects existing in the real world. Such web forums as Studio Wikitecture provide platforms for imaginative expression that benefit amateurs and professionals alike. Studio Wikitecture is an online environment set up to enable avatars to join geographically dispersed design teams and work collaboratively on architecture-based projects. The avatars are free to share ideas, give feedback and contribute to projects initiated by others. Any suggestions for new projects can be reviewed in a context free of preconceptions about how they should be built and inhabited.

A wide variety of consumer goods are now designed and 'manufactured' in virtual worlds, including clothing, furniture and household accessories. These goods are made and exhibited by both design professionals and amateurs. In the future, many virtual products are likely to relate directly to real products, with manufacturers

Researchers at the University of Tokyo are pioneering technology that uses a haptic feedback loop. The technology makes it possible to create pressure sensations on the user's hands, simulating the experience of touching a real object. Here, holographic representations of water drops are 'felt' as they fall into the palm of a researcher's outstretched hand.

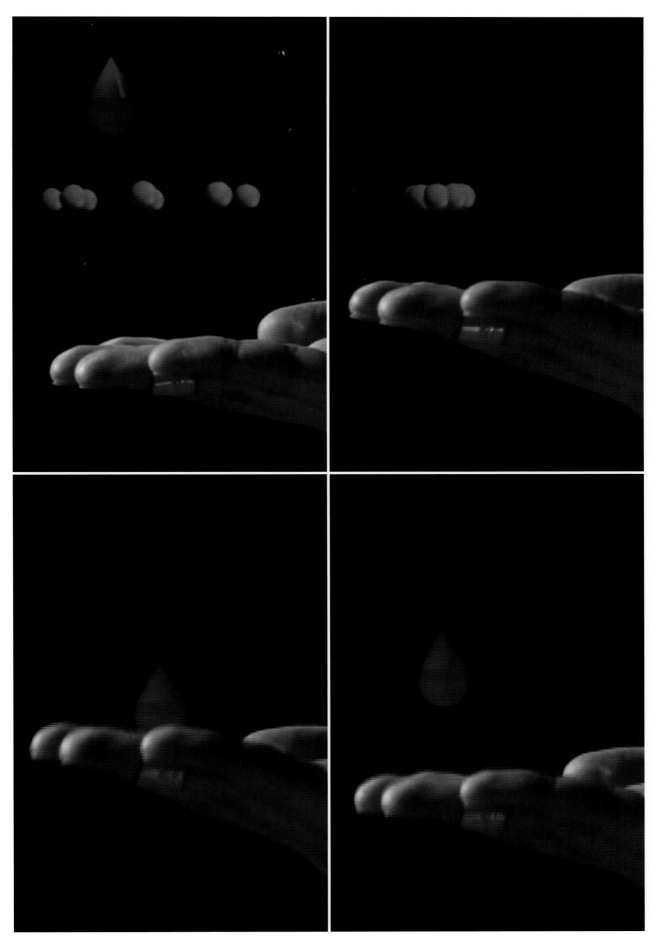

launching both versions at the same time. Virtual products will enable consumers to try out the goods before buying them in real life, and provide them with learning tools that explain and expand the potential uses of the real product.

Virtual products will be significantly enhanced by haptic technology. Combined with virtual-reality software, haptic technology will allow users to engage with virtual objects through their sense of touch, to experience not only the texture but also the weight of an object. Used in conjunction with technology that can represent objects as three-dimensional holograms, haptics will bring a remarkable sense of reality to the act of handling a virtual product. At the University of Tokyo, a team of researchers led by Hiroyuki Shinoda is pioneering technology that uses a haptic feedback loop to create the sensation of pressure on the user's hands. By adding the sense of touch to virtual experiences, the technology gives virtual surfaces a whole new dimension.

The Toyota iQ Interactive Gesture Experience was designed and developed by seeper, the interactive arts and technology collective based in London. The system detects movements directed towards it, and reconfigures itself accordingly. Here, the user is able to displace a series of virtual tiles by waving his or her hands at the screen, which also displays a 'reflection' of the user underneath the tiles.

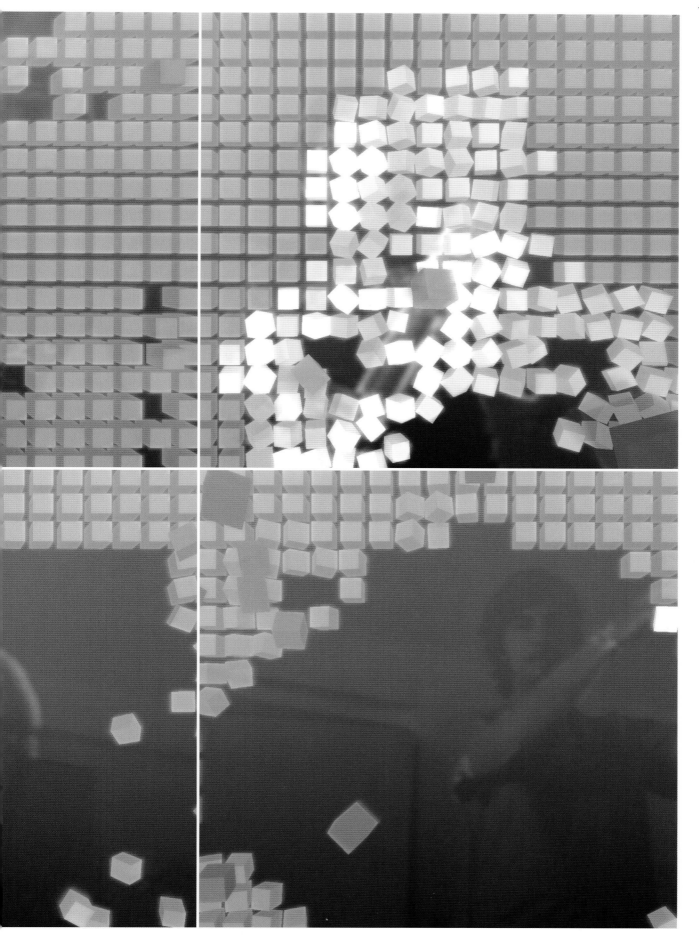

THE INVISIBLE

The very idea of invisible surfaces may seem to be pure fantasy, but the means of making objects vanish from view could appear on the horizon sooner than we think. The dawning of metamaterials, mentioned previously in the 'Mega Materials' chapter (page 101), has already inspired designers and technologists to try to create surfaces that enable light to pass through them. If light can be channelled through a surface or deflected around it, both the surface itself and the structure it covers can be rendered 'invisible'.

Paradoxically, some efforts to create invisible objects are based on new developments in near-infrared (NIR) reflective surfaces and the retro-reflective technology that heightens a surface's visibility. Many of the substances used in the production of NIR materials and infrared filters can be used to create surface coatings that can make an object indiscernible to the naked eye. Polysulfone plastics, for example, which block out 99 per cent of the visible white-light spectrum, form the basis of a coating used to create 'black body' surfaces. The coating masks the energy radiated by the surface to which it has been applied, rendering the surface – and thus the object it is covering – invisible to radar.

For many years, such 'cloaked' surfaces could be found only in the defence industry, which had developed them to make air- and land-borne vessels undetectable by radar. The principles behind cloaking technology have since become available to civilian designers, including Susumu Tachi, the inventor of an 'invisibility' cloak. Tachi, a scientist based at the University of Tokyo, developed a special type of retro-reflective fabric that functions as a photographic screen. He then made a hooded grey overcoat from the fabric, and rigged it with wearable imaging technology that can film and display the wearer's surroundings in real time. An integrated camera records the scene immediately behind the wearer, projecting the images on to the front of the garment. This creates the illusion that the wearer is transparent, since individuals facing him or her are able to see the scene that his or her body would normally block from view. To the naked eye, it is obvious that the wearer is cloaked in imaging technology; seen through a viewfinder, however, the projections on the garment's surface blend seamlessly with their surroundings, creating the impression that the wearer is not there at all.

The surfaces that can be created using such imaging technology have many potential applications, especially in the defence, healthcare, aerospace and textile industries. For example, the technology could lead to an advanced form of military camouflage capable of photographing a soldier's surroundings and digitally transferring the images on to the surface of his or her combat gear. Healthcare specialists claim that surgical gloves made with retro-reflective surfaces could enhance a surgeon's ability to see an incision when it becomes obscured by the surgeon's own hands or equipment. Imaging technology in the palms of the gloves would film the incision and project the images on to the back of the surgeon's hands, effectively making them 'disappear'.

The use of retro-reflective surfaces is also being explored by the aerospace industry. Such surfaces could make the floors of cockpits appear transparent, facilitating smoother landings during difficult conditions. If fitted to architectural surfaces, retro-reflective panels could lend a sense of transparency to a building, or brighten windowless rooms by bringing images of the outside in.

Jane Harris, a British designer, researcher and consultant, uses motion-capture technology to isolate the body's movements, subsequently rendering the body itself invisible. The movements are recorded by a computer, which translates them into a mesh-like digital grid. Harris then uses this grid to simulate the motions of a body inside the virtual textiles she designs.

REACTIVE MEMBRANES

As new technologies equip surfaces with interfaces capable of reacting to their environments, a whole new range of visual and structural effects is beginning to emerge. Robotic membranes that respond to body heat, such as those designed for the Slow Furl project (page 42), will enable walls and furniture to move and change shape, while smart carpets embedded with microelectronics and proximity sensors are able to respond to footsteps. Surfaces coated with multifaceted molecules will form new textures when exposed to electric charges or magnetic fields, making the surfaces abrasion-resistant or even armour-like. Contaminant-aware surfaces will sense environmental toxins and release substances to counteract them, creating biocompatible designs that eliminate bacteria and improve air quality.

These complex surfaces will be activated wirelessly, and will share information and resources with other wireless devices. Finnish technology developer PowerKiss is already forging a new direction for wirelessly activated surfaces by creating systems that recharge electronic gadgets on contact. The company has developed a charging transmitter that can be integrated into furniture surfaces, and a corresponding charging receiver that plugs into electronic devices. As resonating coils embedded in both the transmitter and the receiver begin to respond to one another, they initiate the transmission of a low-voltage electric charge. PowerKiss, which has already added the technology to a conference table and a coffee table made by Martela, is currently talking to mobile-phone companies about building the technology into handsets. It also foresees a day when laptops and other devices will be recharged wirelessly.

A group of Swedish designers has created a reactive tabletop that changes its appearance in response to the conversation around it. Known as Table Talk, the design was created by Marcus Ericsson, David Sjunnesson, John Eriksson and Minna Gedin in order to give furniture a social context rather than a fixed aesthetic. The table responds to speech by assigning colours to the sounds it identifies; these colours appear on the table's surface in real time as the speakers are talking. A glance at the table should reveal the type of social intercourse taking place around it. A pulsating, colourful table, for example, could indicate a lively conversation or heated debate, while a surface showing few colour spots might suggest that those seated around it do not have much to say to one another.

The London-based multi-sensory arts and technology organization known as seeper is pioneering many different types of reactive surface. Among them is a reactive tiling system that provides illumination for public spaces. Each individual tile in the system is capable of detecting changes in light levels; as passers-by draw close to a bank of tiles and cast their shadows over them, the tiles respond by lighting up. The effect is that of creating trails of light through public spaces that map out physical pathways. The tiles' performance can be likened to touch-reactive technology, with movement and gesture taking the place of direct contact. The illuminating surface created by the tiles provides not only a source of light but also a source of fun for the people walking past it. By merging the practical with the whimsical, the tiling system is facilitating a whole new type of user experience. It has already shown how reactive surfaces can

TOP
This interactive multitouch sphere designed by seeper is a groundbreaking three-dimensional surface that enables users to explore new ways of viewing images. Users can also use the sphere to perform such routine tasks as editing documents.

BOTTOM, LEFT AND RIGHT
Finnish technology developer PowerKiss is bridging the gap between wireless devices and energy fields transmitted through everyday surfaces. The firm has developed a charging transmitter that can be integrated into furniture surfaces, and a corresponding charging receiver that plugs into such wireless devices as laptops and mobile phones. When the receiver-enabled device is placed near a transmitter, it begins to recharge.

The creation of a group of Swedish designers, Table Talk is a reactive tabletop that changes the appearance of its surface in response to the conversation around it. As the technology identifies speech patterns, it assigns colours to the sounds it recognizes. The patterns and colourways that take shape in the tabletop's surface reflect the nature of the surrounding conversation.

both inspire individuals to interact with their surroundings and provide an essential means of attracting more human traffic.

Just as ceiling and wall surfaces can detect human movement, reactive floors can sense when someone is walking or standing on them. Future-Shape, a German research organization founded by Christl Lauterbach, has created a reactive, fibre-based underlay that can be placed beneath virtually any type of flooring. Known as SensFloor, the underlay is fitted with a network of integrated sensors that detect movement on the surface above them. When activated by footsteps, the sensors relay location- and time-specific data to a central control unit in real time. SensFloor is equipped with pattern-recognition software that can discern, record and store individual gaits. As well as being able to identify any gait pattern it has previously recorded, the software can detect the presence of an unidentified gait, locate where it entered the system and track its movements. The software is also able to communicate with other systems, to trigger alarms or discreetly alert security staff to the presence of an intruder.

The technology that enables SensFloor to monitor individual gaits makes it suitable for use in certain healthcare applications. When used to monitor a patient's movements remotely, it can identify a fall, or notify carers when an unusually long period of inactivity is detected. The technology can even illuminate embedded LEDs to guide rescuers directly to the person who has fallen. SensFloor can also recognize the gaits of patients with impaired mobility, activating automatic doors and lighting systems as they enter or leave a room.

Patients of every age will benefit from the contaminant-aware surfaces being developed by medical researchers. Surfaces that can detect and neutralize certain bacteria are gaining currency in care facilities, where they are used in conjunction with other antibacterial protocols. Researchers are currently collaborating with technologists on the development of surfaces that discolour when contaminated, providing those present with visual evidence of the appearance of bacteria. Researchers are also developing means of bonding contaminant-aware substances to fibres in order to create bandages that can alert patients to the presence of infectious agents before they become harmful. The Royal College of Art's Visible Invisibility project, run by Anne Toomey, is pioneering a smart bandage that has the look and feel of an ordinary bandage, yet functions as a diagnostic device. The bandage's surface changes appearance when it detects bacteria, revealing alternative motifs and colourways. Each infectious agent triggers a specific colour, enabling the surface to show exactly what kind of infection has been detected.

Wider concerns about the number of environmental contaminants being released in urban centres are motivating designers and urban planners to develop architectural surfaces equipped with sensors capable of monitoring pollution levels. The sensors could be used to activate a warning signal when they detect the presence of airborne toxins, which might otherwise have gone undetected. In theory, the same sensors could also initiate the release of minute particles to neutralize the toxins immediately.

SWITCHABLE SURFACES

Coating an object with a layer of multifaceted molecules gives it a surface that can sense and respond to external stimuli. These molecules are engineered to rotate, ripple or form new configurations when they detect atmospheric changes, magnetic fields or electrical charges. Surfaces made up of these molecules are known as 'switchable', because after the molecules have completed the actions they were triggered to perform, they will automatically switch back to their original configuration.

Robert Langer, a chemical engineer and nanotechnologist based at the Institute for Soldier Nanotechnologies at the Massachusetts Institute of Technology, was one of the first people to explore the potential of 'switchable' technology, engineering a shape-shifting plastic material into switchable fibres. Langer realized that if the colour of a thread could be controlled by an electrical impulse, manipulating the power level could be a means of reconfiguring colourways. Langer used the technology as the basis for a colour-changing textile that can camouflage soldiers as they move through different terrains.

Langer has also created a switchable surface that changes from water-attracting to water-repelling when a low-voltage electric current is applied. The surface is constructed from water-permeable hydrophilic molecules engineered to have a hydrophobic 'back'. The molecules, described as long and lean, are arranged in a self-assembled monolayer that exposes their hydrophilic 'front'. When a positive electrical charge is sent through the layer, the current pulls the top of each molecule downwards, exposing the hydrophobic area covering its back, and rendering the entire surface water-resistant. Once the current has been reversed, the molecules return to their original positions, leaving only their hydrophilic part exposed. If a similar layer of molecules were applied to furniture upholstery, the effect would be that of applying a Teflon-like coating to the fabric. Delicate fibres could display their soft side in normal mode, and then switch over to their tough, stain-resistant side at times when heavy wear-and-tear was anticipated.

As the technology behind switchable surfaces is made compatible with the woven circuits and conductive fibres being developed for interior textiles and fashion applications, such surfaces could be activated automatically by sensors. A summer jacket, for example, could switch to its water-repellent surface when it detects rising levels of humidity – without the wearer noticing any changes at all. Likewise, a garment's fibres could release micro-encapsulated sunscreen in response to sunny weather, or medicate the wearer with transdermal drugs when allergens were sensed in the immediate environment.

Switchable technology relies on shape-shifting materials and conductive fibres that can transmit electrical impulses throughout the surface of an object. Microchips and microcircuits can transmit data and manipulate power frequencies to effect changes in surface textures and reconfigure colourways.

INTERACTIVE TECHNOLOGY

Interactive surfaces can make everyday objects multifunctional and fun. Such reactive technologies as touch-sensitive screens have the potential to turn even the most mundane of objects into a technological interface, enabling designers to take functionality to new heights.

Sam Buxton's Surface Intelligent Objects Table is a dining table with a difference. Instead of a conventional tabletop, the design features a display screen made up of sixty-six illuminating areas that can communicate, display information and react to objects placed on top of them. Buxton has programmed the table with etiquette protocols, enabling it to highlight the areas underneath the appropriate cutlery and glassware each time a new

course is served. By creating information displays on the table's surface, Buxton has given the table the potential to interact with diners as it follows their movements.

While such designs as Buxton's tabletop offer a specific range of integrated functions, other interactive surfaces are able to respond to external electronic devices, including mobile phones, laptops and MP3 players. Atracsys, a technology developer based near Lausanne in Switzerland, has developed a surface that can interact with certain types of electronic device. When one of these devices is placed on the surface, it surrounds the object with displays of multimedia content, such as audio and video files, related to its functions. A mobile phone,

Swiss technology firm Atracsys has created a surface that can interact with certain types of electronic device. When a mobile phone is placed on the surface, for example, it can display the handset's functions and controls (below, left). The user does not need to touch the phone in order to operate it, but can access its functions by tapping on the icons displayed around it. Other devices may trigger the surface to display multimedia content, such as audio and video files related to the device's functions (below and opposite).

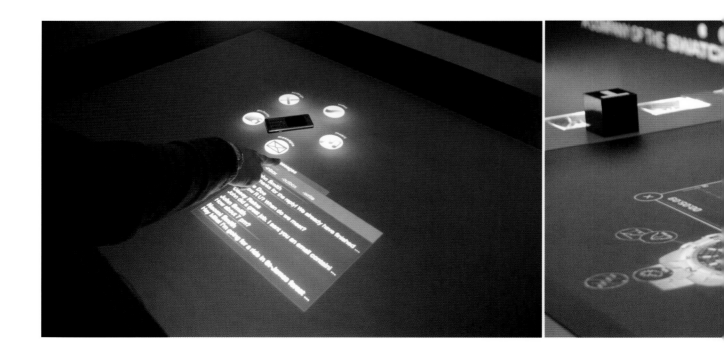

for example, may prompt the surface to show the handset's controls, allowing the user to operate the phone by tapping the icons displayed around it rather than the phone itself.

Interactive surfaces can also be used to create dynamic learning tools. The Virtual Autopsy Table, for example, is an interactive learning device that displays three-dimensional images of the inside of the human body derived from datasets created by CT and MRI scanners. Developed by researchers at the Norrköping Visualization Centre and the Center for Medical Image Science and Visualization at Linköping University, both in Sweden, the system enables users to explore the human body through a multitouch interface that simulates a medical autopsy. The device can also be used by doctors to plan and rehearse complex operations, or to explain medical procedures to patients before surgery.

Interactive technology can also be applied to fabrics and other fibre-based surfaces, enabling them to change colour or reconfigure their patterns and motifs. Electronic fabrics are made with conductive fibres, embedded circuitry and microcontrollers, giving them the potential to form data networks. Maggie Orth, an American textile technologist and founder of the International Fashion Machines research lab, has created a fully interactive textile embroidered with conductive fibres and electronic sensors. Called Petal Pusher, the textile disperses a low-voltage unearthed

electrical charge throughout its surface. When the wearer touches the conductive fibres, the electrical charge is grounded by his or her body, and the textile lights up. As the wearer changes position, his or her contact with the fibres varies, causing the textile to dim and brighten accordingly. As well as controlling the luminosity, the tufted electronic sensors integrated in the textile can activate the appearance of one of forty-nine different patterns. Petal Pusher challenges the notion that a textile's surface motif is a fixed entity, showing that it has the potential to become animate.

Although the touch-screen and multitouch technologies described here are among the most groundbreaking of our time, their operation still requires a certain skill set and physical coordination. Voice-response systems provide a hands-free alternative that is easier to operate. Such systems are controlled by the human voice, allowing users to operate them while using their hands for other tasks. Voice-response technology has advanced quickly in recent years, and the latest voice-operated devices can recognize multiple voices, and accommodate a variety of accents and dialects. They are also able to respond to several commands simultaneously, distinguishing between different voices and even providing verbal feedback – effectively holding a conversation with the user.

Many different devices can be operated by voice commands. Voice-operated telephones and computers, for example, are ideal for users with impaired mobility and those who require a hands-free option in order to multitask. Voice-response systems are also being integrated into household appliances, such as the prototype washing machine invented by German software developer Speech

Experts in partnership with Siemens. The washing machine is intended to be easier to operate than other hi-tech models, and can be spoken to as though it were a human being. When the user describes what type of clothes he or she would like to clean, the machine tells him or her how they should be washed. The washing machine's software includes personality subroutines, so that when it has been told that a garment has been stained with red wine, it may respond by recommending that the user drink beer in future (since beer stains are far easier to remove). Currently, the machine has a vocabulary of several hundred German words, but Speech Experts foresees a version that can understand up to 4000 words in several different languages.

If the surfaces covering machines and products are designed with intelligence and charm, future humans may have to sharpen their conversation skills. Conversing with everyday appliances could turn out to be more stimulating and thought-provoking than making small talk with a human who has nothing interesting to say.

OPPOSITE
Developed by Atracsys, beMerlin is an interactive holographic screen that can be activated without touching it. When the system is used for retail applications, customers can browse the manufacturer's collection simply by twiddling their fingers or by subtly moving their arms.

PAGES 190–91
This enormous structure, some 6 metres (20 feet) high and 8 metres (26 feet) wide, formed part of Canon's NeoReal installation. High-definition images projected on to its surface evoked a chameleon-like organism that constantly changes its skin, as well as creating an immersive kaleidoscope effect.

JANE HARRIS

Jane Harris is a designer, researcher and consultant, and currently holds the position of Professor of Digital Design Imaging at Kingston University, London. Harris was one of the first people to use motion-capture technology to translate the movement of fabric into digital form, taking it far beyond the limitations of the physical world. Her approach to using emerging computer-imaging tools influenced the rendering of materials in early digitally produced films and advertising. Harris is best known for her highly crafted garments and material works that exist solely in the digital realm, the drape and movement of which are extremely lifelike. For Harris, motion-capture technology is an invaluable means of mapping the movements and reflexes of the human body, and she uses the resulting data to drive her ethereal designs. As Harris continues to explore the use of imaging tools in the creation of digital objects, she explains here how her work shows that new paradigms of computer-generated form and surface design are soon to emerge.

What makes virtual surfaces so compelling?

A widespread fascination with virtual worlds generated a drive to make the objects in them look more refined or crafted, to make them look truly believable to the viewer. Material and surface knowledge are key aspects of achieving this. The surface, in our real-life experience, is something we take for granted. As humans, we have a tendency to judge more than merely books by their cover. Our perception of just about everything is informed by exterior skins that determine how things look, our understanding of them, their material construct, behaviour and purpose. Human beings respond to the surface in more ways than we understand consciously. Our initial engagement with an object is often informed by our visual and haptic perception of the surface, followed by a whole range of related experiential references, almost irrespective of an object's form.

What technologies do you use?

The objects I create are developed by exploring the use of 3D computer-graphic animation tooling in animated and real-time contexts. The technologies provide me with tools that enable me to produce garment pieces that are both designed and simulated. This process provides designers and the public with a means of looking at forms in a different way. The term 'virtual' is not perhaps the best term for describing what I do, because it implies a simulation of something we know. Of key interest to me in using these particular imaging technologies is that they give designers some tools to explore things that they don't yet know.

Are digital surfaces perceived differently from real ones?

A digital object can be given any type of surface we can imagine, and some we have yet to conceive of, which means it is possible to experiment with the perception of objects in digital space.

What roles can digitally represented designs play in the future?

Motion-capture tooling combined with the representation of garments using computer graphics could become a part of online shopping, enabling consumers to try on clothes digitally to experience their movement, fit and drape. Interior fabrics could also be tried out digitally, to see how they drape and catch the light. Some objects, such as museum artefacts, are too fragile to be touched, while some are so delicate that they can't even be displayed. Creating virtual representations of these objects allows the public to experience them more fully, since they can be seen and interacted with in ways that the physical objects cannot.

Which aspects of your work can be applied to other design practices?

In many respects, surfacing and surface design are entities unto themselves, yet they have a huge impact on other areas within design. For example, the look and narrative of film, computer games, and the interactive and virtual sectors of the future could evolve in new ways with the development and application of different digital-design aesthetics. This is especially the case as mobile communications systems merge and become almost invisible, increasing not only our mobility but also our engagement with a range of digital spaces, including those designed for entertainment, consumerism or even museum experiences. Elsewhere, by combining body scanning and computer-graphic imaging, it is possible that more consumers may be able to participate in the design of bespoke and couture forms, and, in time, experience fit, drape and movement virtually, enabling them to see how the surface of a material operates in motion.

TOP
One of the applications of Harris's work is the recreation of historic garments that are too fragile to be displayed. Her representations of them enable viewers to see how they would look if actually worn.

CENTRE
Harris's virtual version of the 'balloon' top by British fashion designer Shelley Fox shows how the design changes from a flat, balloon-like form into a three-dimensional garment.

BOTTOM
Harris translates the movement of fabric into digital representations. The garments she creates are entirely virtual, but their drape and movement are lifelike enough for them to seem real.

FREEDOM OF CREATION

While the design lab known as Freedom Of Creation (FOC) is based in Amsterdam, its reputation is worldwide. Founded by Janne Kyttanen in 2000, the lab was established to develop 3D printing processes capable of creating objects designed using 3D modelling software. The 3D printing processes used by FOC include such laser-based technologies as laser sintering and stereolithography, whereby a laser solidifies one tiny layer of material at a time, slowly building up a three-dimensional object. By building up thin 'printed' layers, these processes can create objects inside other objects, objects with deep recesses or undercuts, or objects composed of numerous interlocking forms. Because the processes fabricate an object's inner core and outer layers at the same time, they blur the distinctions between structure and surface. In the following interview, Kyttanen explains that as FOC pioneers new manufacturing technologies, its work is also forging a new role for the surface design of the future.

Which aspects of your work are changing product design and architecture?

In terms of form and function, there is potential for a lot of change. The 3D printing processes I use make it possible to produce forms that would be technically difficult to produce by conventional means. In terms of production and distribution, my products can be bought by anyone anywhere in the world, without any shipping being involved. Since no moulds are needed to produce them, they can be transported digitally and produced locally by individuals.

Will it eventually be possible to produce soft surfaces using 3D printing?

A 'soft surface' is a relative concept. When that question comes up, I usually reply by asking people, 'How soft is diamond dust?' It is a powder, so it's actually very soft, but it can also be incredibly hard. In other words, it's not about the material, but about how you treat it and what you design with it. The same goes for basically any material. Water is very soft, but try waterskiing and falling flat on your face: water feels very hard then. Our halter-neck dress and some of our handbags are constructed from interlinking pieces that bring chain mail to mind. These products are flexible and fluid, and seem soft to most people; but since the individual pieces from which they are made are rigid, they may also seem hard.

What are the future applications of 3D printing processes?

I'd like to get into the 3D printing of buildings in the near future. The technology behind 3D printing can be scaled up to sizes that make it possible to replicate building components and assemble them robotically; architectural structures could then be built without any building equipment or construction workers on site. The 3D printing process would construct the building layer by layer, creating the interior elements and exterior surfaces simultaneously. I think it could be an efficient and environmentally friendly alternative to conventional construction methods.

RIGHT
One of FOC's earliest designs was an interlinking material that mimics chain mail. The material moves and drapes in the same way as a fashion textile, enabling it to be used for clothing and accessories.

OPPOSITE
FOC teamed up with Dutch designer Ted Noten to produce a collection of jewellery. Traditionally, jewellery designers have worked with sculptors and goldsmiths, but today they are just as likely to explore the potential of CAD software and 3D printing technologies.

FUTUR
FRONT

FUELLING THE FUTURE
FUTURE FORECASTING
MEGATRENDS

Interview with
DAVID SHAH
Forecasting text by
LI EDELKOORT

E
ERS

The future of design rests on the objects we live with now, and many of the products, structures and environments surrounding us today are shaping things to come

We think of the future as a phenomenon that will unfold in many years' time, forgetting that it is inextricably linked to things taking place in the present. The future of design rests on the objects we live with now, and many of the products, structures and environments surrounding us today are shaping things to come. Today's lifestyles, interpersonal dynamics and socio-cultural swings are giving rise to the aesthetics and patterns of behaviour that will create the trends of tomorrow. Fashions within architecture and design usually manifest themselves in terms of a visual language, but the ways in which forms are used and buildings actually lived in are harbingers of more profound changes to come.

Although designers and architects are aware of the significance of emerging trends, few are able to predict them before they happen, or gauge what their impact will be. Most practitioners can easily identify the emerging technologies and new materials that will forge fresh directions for design, but are less confident in their ability to recognize other long-term trends, and often overlook the underlying impact that socio-political movements have on their work. While it is true that technology underpins architecture and design today, the forms that result are more strongly influenced by consumer trends, materials innovations and scientific breakthroughs than anything else. These factors, along with socio-economic shifts, are key to anticipating the future of design and architecture.

The recent downturn in the global economy has profoundly affected the future directions of the design disciplines. As retailers placed smaller orders and the construction industry ground to a halt, markets slowed down and jobs disappeared. The design industry has made a slow recovery, and

facing increased competition from the Far East and the emergence of new markets in the West, it has begun to work more closely with local economies. Even big international corporations have begun to embrace 'localism', typically using local materials and craftsmanship to strengthen their appeal to regional audiences. Internet giant Google, for example, encourages its territorial designers to redesign its logo temporarily to mark holidays and special events in the domains it serves. China's emergence as a significant economic force presents new realities for global trade, with East and West clashing over cultures, ideologies, economics and diplomacy. The resulting cultural-economic battle taking shape within design promises to gain momentum as time goes on.

Yet, paradoxically, even as designers and architects commit to thinking 'local', they continue to be faced with global issues. Climate change is influencing architecture and urban planning throughout the world, and threats to the planet's biodiversity are being addressed by designers working both locally and internationally. The reach of the technologies known as GRIN – genetics, robotics, information technology and nanotechnology – is worldwide, and they are aligning design with science. Along with nanotechnology, neurotechnology and genomics (the study of genomes) are forging links between healthcare, longevity medicine and product design, creating a powerful triumvirate that will radically alter the lifestyle sector of the future.

Biotechnology is a source of innovation in materials science, product design and medicine; it also provides a basis for the development of new fuels to power the buildings and products of the

Concerns over sustainable energy loom large in many debates about future design, making power sources an important consideration for new projects. Designed by Canadian design studio Molo, the Cloud Softlight shown here is illuminated by low-energy LEDs, which are making great advances in terms of efficiency.

future. New sources of energy – such as hydrogen, piezoelectricity (generated when certain materials are subjected to mechanical stress) and waterborne single-celled microalgae – will play a critical role in the future, inspiring new paradigms of product design and architecture based on integrated power sources. And once objects and buildings begin to power themselves, they will also have the ability to self-replicate, curbing the influence exerted by manufacturers. Although ideas, designs and prototypes may continue to be generated elsewhere, the manufacturing process will be local.

In addition to the factors that will determine how future designs are powered and produced, changes in group dynamics will radically alter how products are designed and consumed. A shift from individualism to collectiveness will give rise to new kinds of workforce and different types of labour exchange, which will be more diverse than we can imagine today. Co-workers may not ever share the same physical space, but will be interconnected as if they were working in the same location. Virtual-reality platforms will be the standard means by which colleagues and associates interact with one another, as well as interface with consumers.

The shift from individualism to collectiveness will challenge the power of institutions, governments and corporations. Equally significantly, it will cause a collapse of boundaries within industry, enabling new multidisciplinary areas to emerge. The collaborative efforts between designers and practitioners in different fields that we deem to be 'crossovers' today will be the norm in the future, giving all sectors of industry a voice within design. Most influential of all will be trend experts and future forecasters. Such individuals will come to exert unprecedented power within design, not because they can actually foresee the changes to come, but because their work – the generation of concepts, 'mood boards' and inspirations, for example – bridge the ever-widening gap between physical products and virtual designs.

The remainder of this chapter outlines some of the major determinants of the future of design and architecture. Concerns over sustainable energy loom large in many debates about design, and several new energy sources are detailed in the first section, 'Fuelling the Future'. The subsequent sections provide some insights into the future-forecasting industry, revealing how important it will be for designers to be able to anticipate future trends. At the end of the chapter, a text written by Li Edelkoort and an interview with David Shah reveal some of the future trends within design and architecture.

In addition to bringing a new
type of porosity to the built
environment, architectural
mesh can be used as a light-
diffusing barrier to decrease
light pollution in walkways,
parking garages, balconies and
other types of open structure.
Interwoven LEDs can be
orientated to point inwards
to prevent light from shining
beyond the mesh.

FUELLING THE FUTURE

The industrialized world is rapidly moving away from fossil fuels and towards a new paradigm of carbon-free energy, leading designers to wonder how their products will be powered in the decades ahead. Future energy supplies will be generated by biofuel, biomass, solar energy, geothermal energy, and wind and water turbines, and will be channelled through networks of smart micro- and mini-grids. These networks will break free of the centralized power grids we use today, enabling individual buildings to use alternative energy sources or generate their own. Buildings will not be alone in producing enough energy to operate the systems and appliances within them; electronic devices and portable products will be also designed with integrated power systems.

The human body is in itself a power system, but until recently it had not been widely recognized as an energy source. Normal bodily movements, such as walking, stretching and breathing, can generate enough power to recharge a mobile phone. Aerobic activities, such as cycling, jogging and dancing, can produce enough kinetic energy to power much larger devices. Electricity generated in this way is known as piezoelectricity. Researchers based at the University of California, Berkeley, are developing unobtrusive methods of harnessing the body's kinetic energy. The research team claim that weaving microscopic piezoelectric fibres into a garment could convert physical movement into energy, and that a shirt consisting of 1 million piezoelectric fibres could generate enough energy to operate an MP3 player. A pair of piezoelectric gloves could harness the energy generated by typing at a keyboard, and relay it to the computer's main power source. Researchers at Princeton University and the California Institute of Technology have taken a more extreme approach, maintaining that tiny piezoelectric chips could be surgically implanted in the body to harness the energy created by such involuntary actions as the beating of the heart and the contraction of the lungs.

Piezoelectric chips can also be embedded in membranes outside the body, such as silicone rubber sheets. As the sheets flex under pressure, mechanical stress is applied to the silicone, which generates an electric field in response. The energy that results is absorbed by the chips and relayed as a power source. The Dutch enterprise known as Sustainable Dance Club has created a piezoelectric underlay for dance floors, which converts the energetic movements of dancers into electricity. The technology developed by Sustainable Dance Club has been put into practice in the French city of Toulouse, where officials have embedded kinetic energy pads into pavements to test their ability to power street lights.

Piezoelectric technology is also being applied to sports shoes, in the form of lightweight, pliable mini-generators that can be inserted into the heels of the shoes. The generators, developed by Ville Kaajakari, a researcher based at the University of Louisiana, convert the movements of the shoes' wearer into electricity, either for direct use or for storage in batteries. Kaajakari claims that the generators can produce up to 10 milliwatts of power each as the wearer is pounding the pavements.

In the coming years, much of our energy may be supplied by power plants designed to convert refuse into electricity. Waste2Tricity, an international energy consortium, is pioneering methods of generating electricity from carbon-based

TOP
This studio and exhibition pavilion was designed by R&Sie(n) for Thai artist Rirkrit Tiravanija. Situated in northern Thailand, the building is able to generate its own electricity with the aid of an 'animal engine', a water buffalo harnessed to the wooden turbines shown here. One animal can generate enough energy to recharge several mobile phones and power ten light bulbs and a laptop.

BOTTOM LEFT
As people become more aware of energy consumption, architects and designers are making the mechanics of power production and energy storage more visible.

BOTTOM RIGHT
Parametric lighting can illuminate an entire interior with only one light source, maximizing the amount of ambient lighting in relation to the energy expended.

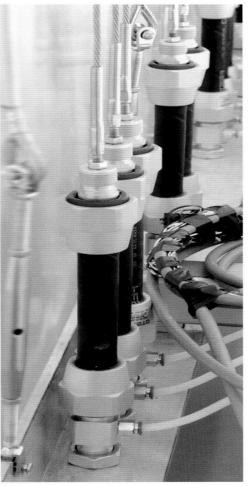

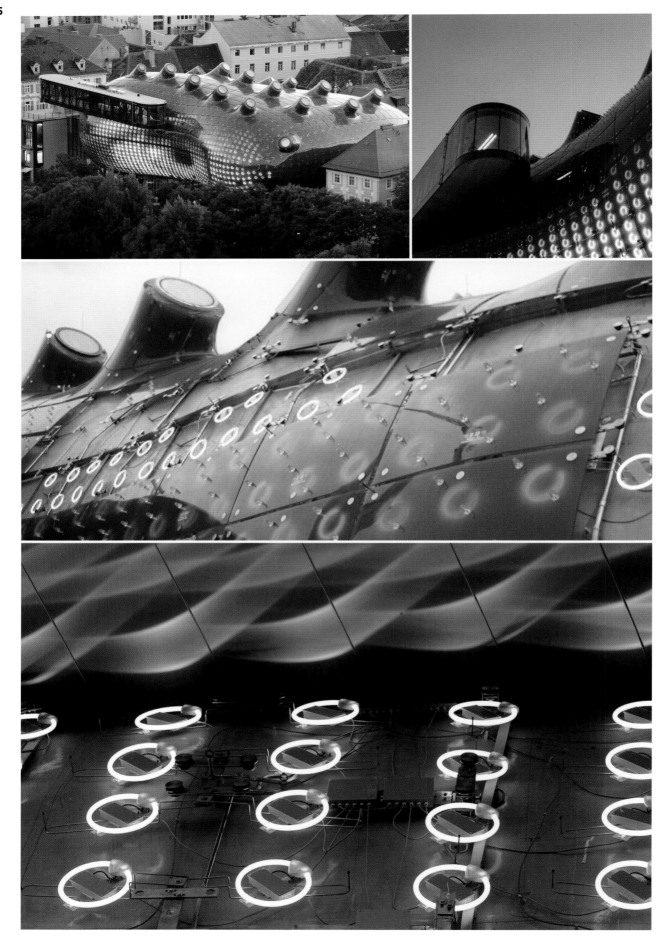

Completed in 2003, the Kunsthaus Graz in Austria was designed by Peter Cook and Colin Fournier. The contemporary architecture stands in dramatic contrast to the surrounding landscape of historic buildings. In addition to featuring systems that conserve energy and generate power, the building boasts a new type of façade. Known as BIX, the façade consists of a Plexiglas skin embedded with fluorescent rings. These rings function as pixels, and can be used to display text and images.

waste and organic refuse. The waste is placed in a plasma gasification chamber, where it is heated to more than 6000°C (10,800°F) and turned into synthetic gas. The gas is then converted into hydrogen, which, in turn, is used to produce electricity via alkaline fuel cells. The waste used in the process can be taken from the millions of tonnes of biomass dumped in landfill each year, transforming a possible environmental hazard into a valuable fuel source.

Hydrogen can be derived from many kinds of waste, making it a potential source of sustainable energy. As refuse starts to break down, it releases concentrations of methane, water, carbon monoxide, carbon dioxide and hydrogen; the hydrogen can then be converted into electricity. Pure hydrogen can also be extracted from water, and blended with other types of fuel to boost supplies. This process is of particular interest to car manufacturers, which would like to make the use of hydrogen more widespread in order to cut fuel emissions. OM Energy, an energy start-up based in Oxford, has developed an electro-hydrogen generator (EHG) for the automobile industry that uses electrolysis to extract hydrogen from water. The hydrogen is then mixed with the vehicle's fuel supply. Trials indicate that the EHG can reduce emissions by 30 per cent, and increase fuel efficiency by 20 per cent, enabling the car to go further on a single tank of petrol.

A global hydrogen economy is proposed by energy experts who regard hydrogen as a fuel of the future for a wide variety of vehicles, from ships and aeroplanes to all forms of public transport. Being an energy carrier, in the same way as electricity, rather than a primary energy source, as in the case of fossil fuels, hydrogen has the potential to reduce

demand on traditional energy sources. Hydrogen occurs naturally only in small quantities, so in order for it to be a viable alternative to energy derived from fossil fuels, it would have to be produced on a large scale using an energy source that was itself sustainable. Those advocating a worldwide hydrogen economy argue that, overall, hydrogen used in transport applications would be less harmful to the environment than petrol, since it does not emit pollutants or carbon dioxide at the point of use.

Today, hydrogen production is already a large and growing industry. Globally, around 50 million tonnes of hydrogen (roughly equivalent to the amount of energy released by burning 170 million tonnes of oil) are produced annually, and the figures continue to rise. Initiatives to produce hydrogen biologically have led to the development of fermentative hydrogen production processes, which use fermentation to convert such organisms as algae and bacteria into biological hydrogen. Biohydrogen, as it is known, can also be produced in an algae bioreactor, in which algae is manipulated to produce hydrogen rather than oxygen. Some bioreactors are able to produce hydrogen from organic waste.

Algae is rich in nutrients and abundant in watercourses throughout the world, and research indicates that, in the future, it could be used to produce biofuel. In a study conducted by the US Department of Energy in New Mexico, researchers were able to harvest biofuel from single-celled microalgae grown in pond water. The biofuel synthesized from the algae is biodegradable and lead-free, emitting two-thirds less carbon dioxide than petrol. Tests showed that the biofuel could power a diesel engine. When compared to the established biofuel-producing crops grown today, algae require much less space to produce the same yield.

Many different sources of energy can be derived from water. The ocean is expected to be a key source of hydroelectric power in the future, with turbines harvesting the energy contained in underwater currents. Researchers at NASA have found another means of harnessing the ocean's energy, by adapting existing thermal-energy conversion technology for use in sub-aquatic depths. NASA's SOLO-TREC underwater vehicle, an unmanned robotic probe used to take readings of ocean currents and salinity levels several hundred metres beneath the surface, is designed to make use of the temperature differences between the cold depths of the ocean and the warmer currents above. The vehicle is fitted with oil-filled tubes surrounded by wax, similar to the heat-exchange technology used in refrigerators and air conditioners. When the vehicle comes into contact with warm water, the wax liquefies and expands, forcing the oil into a high-pressure chamber; the pressurized oil then drives a battery-charging generator. Once the descending vehicle reaches cooler water, the wax solidifies, and the process is repeated as it ascends to warmer temperatures.

Recent advances in wind turbines have exchanged bulky rotating arms for sleek spinning blades that revolve around a vertical axis. Such designs are more efficient, as they can generate electricity irrespective of the direction of the wind. The perfectly proportioned RevolutionAir energy turbines designed by Philippe Starck for Pramac can harness multidirectional airflows silently and discreetly. The turbines' compact size and efficient

design make them ideal for urban environments, where they can easily be fitted to rooftops or installed in parks.

Another innovative wind turbine has dispensed with blades altogether. The Fuller Wind Turbine, the creation of New Hampshire-based Solar Aero Research, is fitted with a series of thin discs. Wind passing over the rims of the discs produces considerable amounts of drag, which is then used to drive the internal generator. The Fuller Wind Turbine has several advantages over conventional turbines, the blades of which often create noise, generate radar interference and invariably injure wildlife.

Energy can be derived from surprising sources, and the drive to create self-powered products is likely to inspire designers to explore unconventional materials. As piezoelectric technology takes hold, bodies and buildings may interface in new ways to share the energy stored in the chips embedded in them. Waste will become a thing of the past, with refuse reconceived as an energy source. Water and wind will no longer be regarded as elements of nature alone, but will come to be seen as unlimited sources of power for an unlimited range of designs.

Philippe Starck's RevolutionAir wind turbines for Pramac use sleek spinning blades rather than bulky rotating arms. The blades rotate around a vertical axis, enabling them to generate electricity irrespective of the direction of the wind.

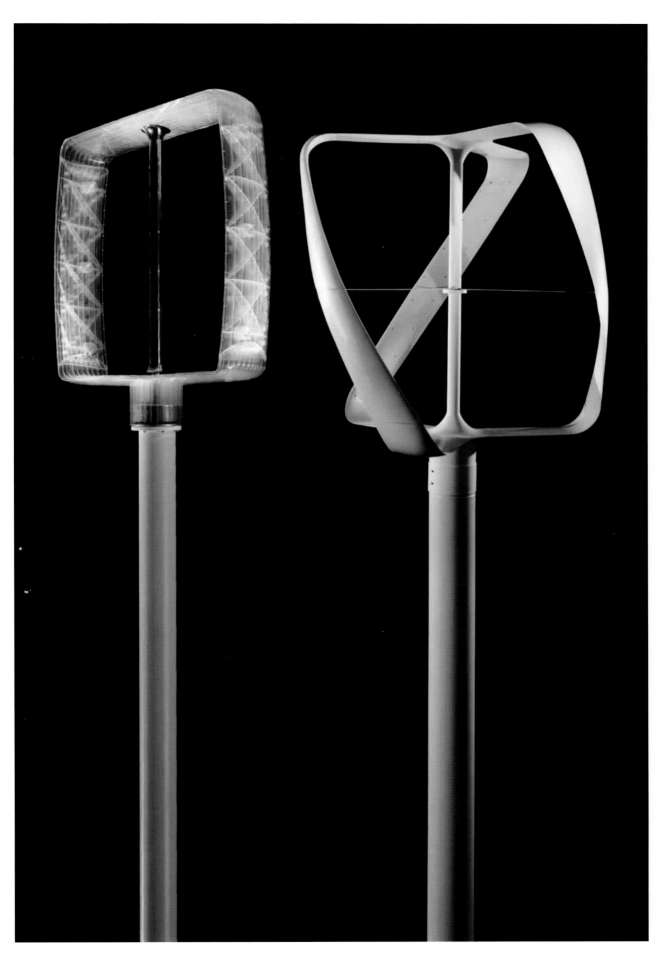

FUTURE FORECASTING

Wondering how life will take shape in the future has preoccupied the civilized world for countless generations; speculating on what lies ahead even seems to be part of what makes us human. History has shown how homes, furniture, clothes and household objects can change dramatically from one generation to the next, and how aesthetic movements can come to characterize whole lifestyles. Although the inevitability of change challenges all of us to imagine what lies ahead, only a handful of individuals dare to identify emerging trends and predict in which directions they will go. Future forecasters and trend experts follow emerging shifts in many sectors, so when questions are asked about the future of design, they are the ones with the answers.

The foundations of future forecasting were laid in the mid-nineteenth century when French philosopher Auguste Comte predicted the emergence of the social sciences; subsequently, these foundations gave rise to the practice of trend analysis that gained popularity in the 1960s. Since then, relatively few trend forecasters have had a lasting impact on the design industry. Li Edelkoort and Faith Popcorn burst on to the scene in the 1980s, providing intuitive projections for aesthetic trends and lifestyle shifts. Edelkoort understood that anticipating aesthetic trends and adapting to societal shifts lie at the very heart of design, and by the end of the 1980s her inspirational trend concepts had begun to gain currency among practitioners in fashion, design, interiors and architecture. In the 1990s, Promostyl, Future Concept Lab and the Future Laboratory introduced a somewhat more ethnographic approach, tracking worldwide changes in visual culture and predicting their impact on design-conscious consumers. The combined efforts of these practitioners, together with theorists active within the discipline of future studies, have revolutionized the ways in which architecture and design are conceived and created. Whereas practitioners once designed forms with today's consumers in mind, now they create designs for the markets soon to emerge.

Many professionals working at the top end of design subscribe to forecasting publications, buy trend books or even commission bespoke future concepts from leading forecasters. This often gives them a competitive advantage over others in the industry, as expert knowledge enables designers to differentiate between long- and short-term transformations, and distinguish a hunch from a bona fide trend. Forecasters maintain that a lasting trend will have had a certain amount of coverage in various media, and that, in the case of surveys, most individuals will acknowledge it as an accepted value, a mode of behaviour or an identifiable product. Forecasters generally claim that when 15 to 25 per cent of a given population has incorporated an innovation, action or belief into its normal lifestyle, it can then be acknowledged as a mainstream trend.

As professional forecasters mediate between the future and the present, they identify the recurrence of aesthetic cycles, recognize patterns in consumer behaviour and make projections that form the basis for long-range forecasts. Although each has an individual perspective, most forecasters work with concepts that relate in some way to the global shifts known as 'megatrends'. Megatrends are derived from such factors as economic growth, lifestyle shifts, technological advances and the

Future fashion trends include garments that can light up, change colour or display animated motifs. The Frison bodysuit by Philips Design shown here is a uniquely responsive garment that reacts to movement around it by illuminating and blinking.

availability of natural resources. Information about megatrends is available in the public domain, and practitioners working with architecture and design generally gauge an awareness of them from news reports and other media coverage of current events. More specific trends can be monitored by following new developments in the media, or by routinely logging on to trend-watching websites. Some internet forums encourage individual users to contribute to their content, providing trend researchers with fresh data from which they can identify new developments, while others attempt to monitor trends through algorithms built into their electronic databases.

Although designers and architects are not generally motivated by trends *per se*, their work often plays an active role in creating them. The aesthetic expressions and functional forms they create can spark new trends by initiating interdisciplinary collaborations and challenging conventional thinking. An awareness of trends enables design practitioners to gauge the market for their products and release them on time, giving the practitioners a uniquely competitive advantage.

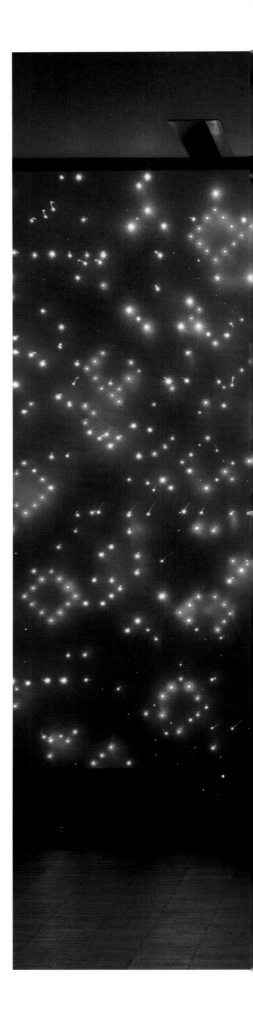

Danish designer Astrid Krogh creates light tapestries made from optical fibres that slowly change colour. Called Morild, this design was inspired by the sea's shimmering appearance, which sometimes looks as though it is being created by tiny lights floating beneath the surface of the water.

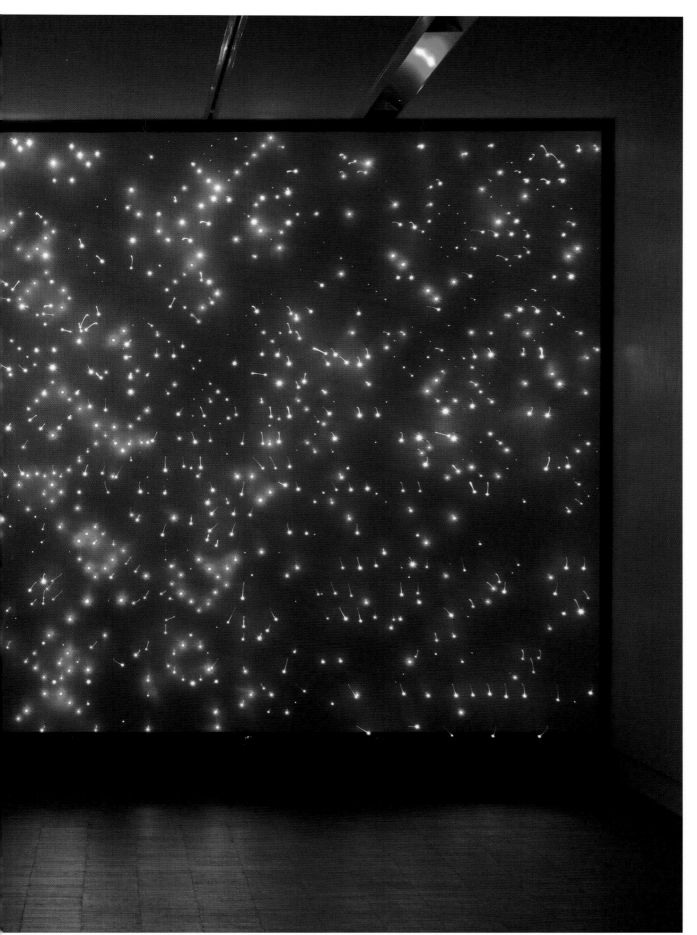

MEGATRENDS

Gaining an awareness of megatrends enables architects and designers to understand better the complex interactions and societal shifts shaping the future of design. Understanding the shifts that each megatrend represents helps practitioners to anticipate what will come next, and even to draw strategic conclusions about the steps to be taken today. Future forecasters have identified a number of megatrends shaping the future, some of which are particularly relevant to the design disciplines. Twelve of these megatrends are listed below, together with summaries of how they are sparking new directions in architecture and design.

Viewed collectively, these megatrends reveal that architecture and design are changing and evolving at a faster pace now than at any time in the past. The design disciplines are undergoing a historic transformation, and as practitioners move forward armed with knowledge of the shifts that are helping to shape the industry, they will become pivotal forces in creating a better future.

Alliances of Cultural Creatives

The term 'cultural creatives' was coined by Paul H. Ray and Sherry Ruth Anderson in their book *The Cultural Creatives: How 50 Million People Are Changing the World* (2000). The term is used by the book's authors to describe an emerging group of influential thinkers, including artists, writers, musicians, theorists and therapists. Significantly, Ray and Anderson also include designers and architects in this group. The authors' recognition that designers and architects coexist within a larger creative sphere points to the fact that their exposure to ideas not traditionally circulated among their ranks is increasing. This paves the way for a future of interdisciplinary platforms, in which people from a wider range of professional affiliations have a voice within architecture and design. These individuals will amass 'cultural capital', which will replace the prestige associated with high salaries and social class. Overall, architecture and products will be more democratic, and not stratify and divide sections of society to the extent that they do today.

Artificial Intelligence

Intelligent agents – autonomous systems able to perceive their surroundings and respond to them – are programmed to work towards achieving goals set by humans. Technological systems can maintain objectivity, and process more information than the human brain, making them efficient alternatives to manpower. In the service industries, for example, humans will be superseded by virtual equivalents, which will deal with enquiries, provide information and solve problems. Individual products and extensive systems will be designed with characteristics that make them appear empathetic, while interactive products will feature preprogrammed 'personalities' instead of the user manuals and online tutorials we use today.

PAGES 216–17
Science and design are
beginning to merge, and
together they may form a
new discipline. Providing
cost-effective, sustainable
healthcare is a central concern
for all medical institutions,
and advances in scanning
technology will enable
doctors to diagnose and
treat illnesses earlier than
is currently possible.

Collective Consciousness

Thanks to the internet and the accessibility of communications technologies, the human race today is more interconnected than ever before. As these technologies continue to evolve, people will be increasingly likely to do things in groups, whether physically or online. Globalization is uniting a diverse range of cultures, and as individuals live longer, healthier lives, people of all ages are transcending generation barriers. Future humans will move from individualism to collectiveness, creating an entirely new society as a result. As they do so, factors related to sex, age, culture and creed will unite individuals rather than divide them. Ideas will be shared and circulated more widely than they are today, and theoretical constructs will be considered to be an essential part of general knowledge.

Dematerialization

Sparked by the drive to make product design more sustainable, the concept of dematerialization (also known as immaterialization) describes the move towards consuming data in alternative ways. For example, maps can viewed online and downloaded into portable devices rather than bought in paper form. E-tickets are putting an end to printed versions, and online transport timetables are eliminating the need for leafy brochures. Because dematerialization represents the replacement of one type of activity with another, it can be said to constitute a lifestyle shift.

Dynamic Well-being

Breakthroughs in geriatrics and advances in the emerging field of longevity medicine mean that, in the years ahead, people will live for longer and enjoy a better quality of life. The spry seniors of the future will continue to relate to youth culture in their later years. As a result, the young and the aged will be more closely aligned than ever before. With good health and anti-ageing treatments of great importance to consumers of all ages, designers and architects will incorporate self-diagnostic devices and medicating technologies into everyday forms. Consumer products will therefore perform the routine duties previously carried out by medical technicians. This will change the way in which the whole health industry operates, promoting well-being rather than scaring consumers into taking preventive medicine they may not need.

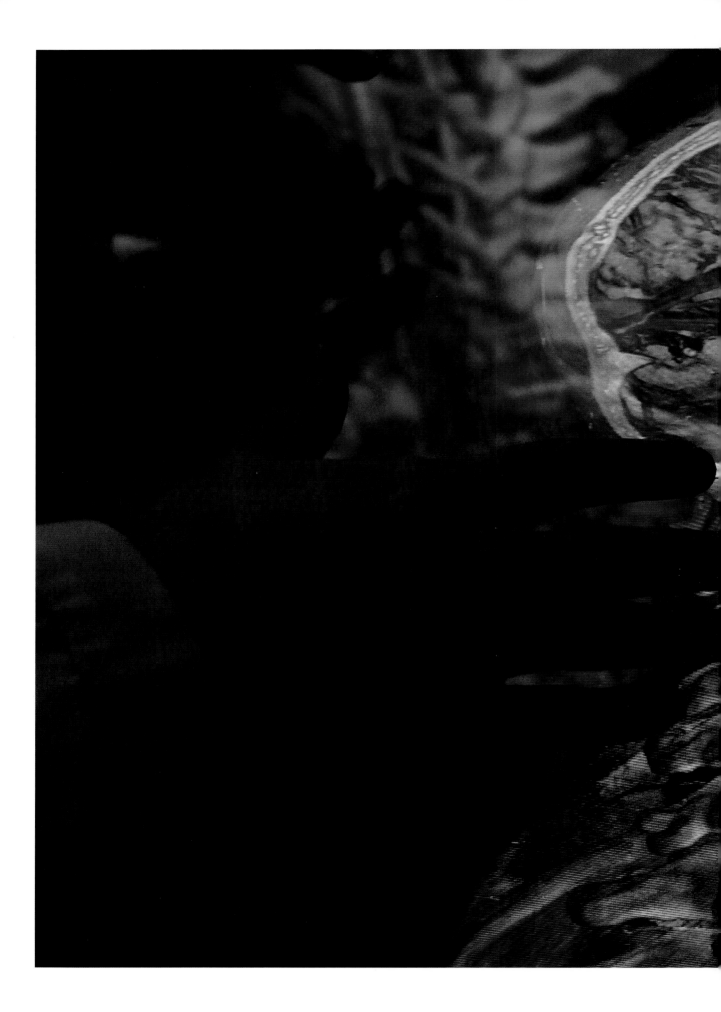

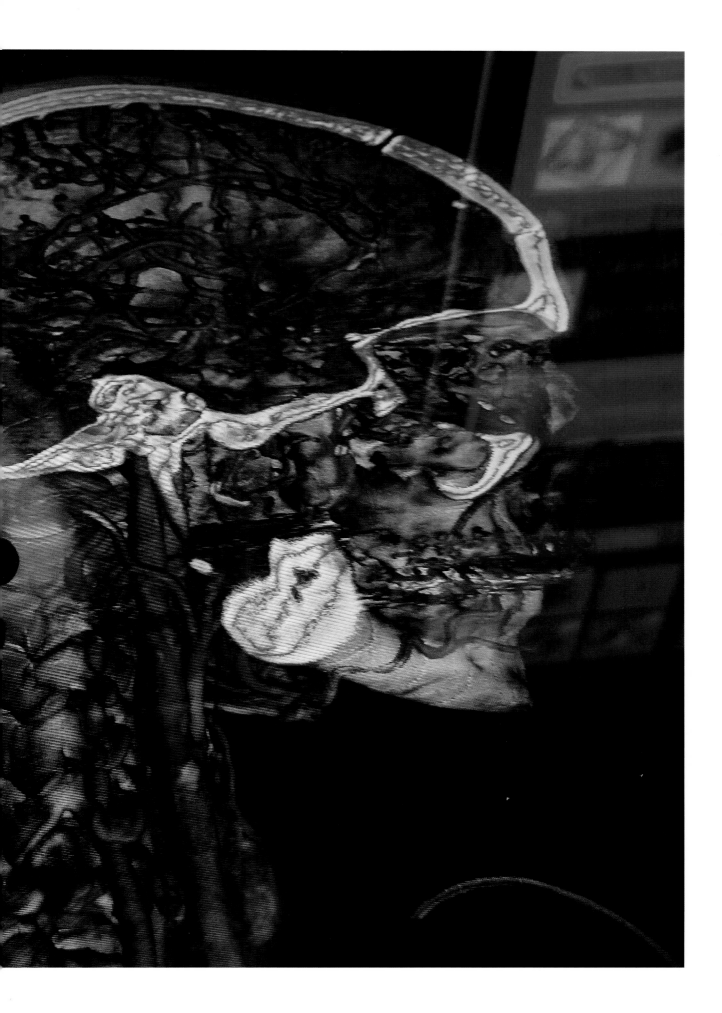

Future humans will be less likely to rely on centralized power grids, ultimately shifting the production of energy to individuals or groups. In places where generators were once required, portable wind turbines could be used instead.

New Energy

As detailed at the beginning of this chapter (page 204), some future fuels will be derived from surprising sources. The drive to create self-powered products and low-energy appliances will reduce the reliance on centralized grids, and will ultimately bring the production of energy under the control of the individual. Photovoltaic cells, wind turbines and micro-hydro electricity offer alternatives to drawing power from existing energy grids, and promise to be complemented by the new fuel sources being pioneered today. In addition, the drive to make all power-consuming products generate their own power will drastically alter the way in which product designers and industrial manufacturers view energy sources.

Self-Replication

Advances in technology mean that some machines now have the ability to produce copies of themselves. Self-replicating devices will make many types of manual labour redundant, improving efficiency and productivity as a result. As consumers begin to own and operate self-replicating machines, they will also be able to customize the products they replicate. This will mean that the designer will no longer be the sole author of the product. Not all goods will be able to be replicated by the consumer; new models of advanced technical devices, for example, will be hired until the replication technology is made available to consumers. The ease with which consumers will be able to manufacture and recycle products portends a new design economy based on abundance rather than scarcity.

Super Science

The scientific method, arguably one of the main driving forces behind the creation of the modern world, will continue to lead to new discoveries. Scientific breakthroughs in such fields as nanoscience, genetics and biochemistry have led to numerous innovations in design, all of which have been assessed with the aid of scientific methodology. As innovative hybrids of science and design emerge in the years ahead, they will be validated according to the natural and physical laws described by the relevant scientific disciplines. Such professions as healthcare, agriculture, design and architecture will change dramatically as they begin to work more closely with science, perhaps even becoming scientific disciplines in their own right. The field of biomimicry, for example, incorporates elements of design in order to create consumer products, but the know-how behind them is rooted in natural science.

As initiatives to establish colonies on other planets gain momentum, vehicles similar to this Mars Exploration Rover are being designed to appraise extraterrestrial resources. Metals and minerals from outer space may one day be harvested for use on Earth.

Sustainable Futures

Regarded by many future forecasters as all-pervasive, the drive towards sustainability is one of the most dominant trends in design and architecture today. Irrespective of designers' world views or aesthetic leanings, the movement to make all forms environmentally friendly has given birth to new paradigms of design. The need to make decisions today in order to protect the environments of the future has transformed the way in which designers and architects relate to materials, processes, societal norms and nature itself. Sustainability is no longer a simplistic model for producing eco-friendly products, but a paradigm of design that incorporates technological and cultural change. With sustainability comes a renewed appreciation of craftsmanship (see page 155); in the future, handcrafted objects will be the ultimate in luxury goods.

Technological Singularity

The efficient management of planetary resources requires a global technological platform that can be shared and accessed by individuals around the world. In the future, a single information system will be developed to meet the needs of a global population and monitor the effects of regional changes on global markets. This system will comprise a range of immersive technological networks that will also shape the lives of future humans as they cocoon themselves in technological 'bubbles' of digital information. Mobile phones, media players, laptop computers and other types of portable device will be integrated into items of clothing and worn on the body or implanted within it, meaning that the wearers will be almost permanently online. While the goal today is the convergence of many platforms, in the future only one platform will exist. The way in which individuals are granted access to it will shape the way they interact with their surroundings and with one another.

Urban Agronomics

As outlined in the 'Urban Utopias' chapter, future food production will no longer be the preserve of rural farmers; instead, it will constitute an essential part of urban life. Areas of public space will be given over to agriculture, forming part of the public sector alongside health, education, the economy and waste treatment. The cultivation of crops will be a consideration for architects and planners alike, who will design and orientate buildings according to their agricultural yield. Agriculture will be an integral part of urban infrastructures and local economies, even to the extent that supermarkets and restaurants will be heavily taxed for importing produce from other municipalities.

Virtual Workforces

E-mail and telecommunications have proven to be poor substitutes for face-to-face communication. Although they can connect people separated by great distances, they rarely foster the interpersonal dynamics generated by people working in proximity to one another. The important non-verbal cues created by body language, tone of voice and personal style are lost when no visual contact is possible, but simulations of such cues can be generated in virtual-reality forums. Virtual workers, represented by avatar-like forms, can even create 'improved' versions of themselves to handle the tasks at hand more effectively. Projections about the workforces of the future maintain that they must embrace innovation if they are to remain competitive in the global, multicultural markets coming into existence. Virtual workers can correct some of the shortcomings of their physical masters, and provide a friendlier, more efficient service as a result.

Imaging and touch-activated technologies are changing the way in which the human body is investigated and how surgery is performed. The Virtual Autopsy Table is a state-of-the-art medical visualization tool with a multitouch interface that enables users to access datasets created by CT and MRI scanners.

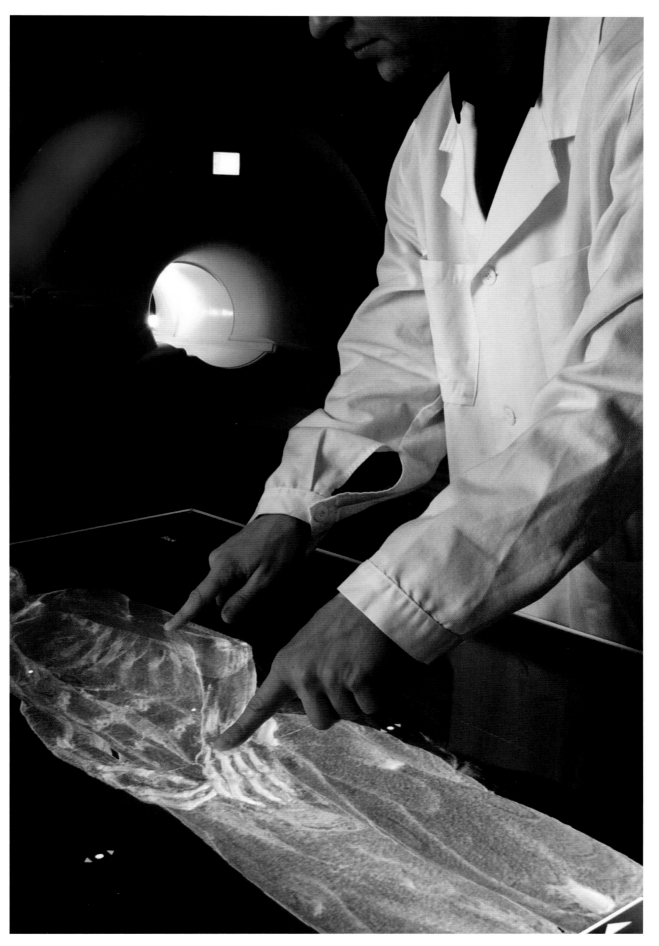

DAVID SHAH

A man known for his expertise in spotting emerging consumer trends, international branding consultant and futurist David Shah has a knack for anticipating new directions in design. Born in Britain but now based in Amsterdam, Shah pursued a career in journalism before launching the influential forecasting publications *Textile View*, *View2* and *Viewpoint*, which he still edits today. Shah, in common with the magazines he founded, has a worldwide following and an authoritative view on many aspects of design. Interviewed exclusively for this book, Shah explains how current exchanges between manufacturer and consumer are forging future pathways for product design.

Will consumers play a key role in shaping design's future?

Big shifts are already emerging within consumers themselves. They are busy wresting control of their own lifestyles and purchasing decisions from marketeers, celebrity-based media and insensitive corporations. A new understanding of what 'value' and 'values' truly mean makes companies realize that they now need to listen to, form relationships with and talk to their customers. Designers are aware that we live in a participatory culture, in which we all contribute and feel socially connected, living increasingly creative lives. The brands for which designers work are now expected to behave like individuals, moving from a model that was once 'transactional' to one that is now about what Henry Jenkins, a professor of communications at the University of Southern California, calls the three Cs: conversation, collaboration and creation. As consumers buy small stakes in a brand, the emergence of partnership branding gives the consumers not only a sense of empowerment but also a better sense of true value.

What changes will occur in retail?

Such budget retailers as Poundland, Primark, Aldi and Asda are growing rapidly, and will continue to do so, while prestigious brands will launch cheaper private labels. Consumers are increasingly choosing a product packaged in no-nonsense, straight-talking graphics, which reassure them that they are paying for content, not image. Designers and manufacturers should be made aware that thrift is a key factor in current buying decisions. This new frugality, seen particularly among today's middle class, is not a temporary reaction to the economic slump, but a long-term mind-shift underlining the 'new normal'. This is due partly to personal desire, and partly to financial necessity. With this frugality comes a new 'voluntary simplicity' movement, where the aim is to cut back on material possessions. Services are springing up to help people sell excess household items. This movement is paralleled by a new desire to 'make do and mend', with sales of sewing machines, haberdashery and thrifty cookery books all booming. Consumers now exchange goods at 'swap parties', and in the future are increasingly likely to barter for services and goods.

Will consumers shop differently in the future?

In the years to come, retailing will become almost fully automated, thanks not only to improving wireless technologies but also to the use of RFID [radio-frequency identification] chips. Customers will be given a small scanning device, and instead of asking for help from a shop assistant, they will flash the device at the desired item, and information will appear on the device's screen, displaying the colours and sizes available together with images of models wearing the same garment. There will, of course, also be suggestions about other products to buy – accessories or matching items of clothing, for example. Should the desired item not be in stock or the size not be available, the device will tell you where the nearest available purchase point is, or offer to send it to you later or bring it in from another store. There will be 'magic mirrors' with push-touch controls that enable you to try on clothes, try out different make-up colours *etc.* at the push of a button, and even social-network devices to connect you to friends so that they can see the product on you and give an opinion.

How significant will DIY design be in the future?

Whether you realize it or not, we are already living in a do-it-yourself society; in the future, we are likely to do even more things for ourselves. Once, there were polite cashiers, staff and experts available to help us. Now, we face impersonal machines with a logic that, if not followed correctly, drives you to insanity as you input information again and again. We withdraw and pay in our money at cash machines rather than with the help of a bank cashier; we check out and bag our own grocery items; we check ourselves in for flights; and we are increasingly invited to design our own garments and our own products. DIY design may present big problems, however, as it replaces design professionals with amateurs. Because experts seem expensive, Mr and Mrs Bloggs think they can save money by doing it themselves. Take designing your own clothes, for example. Everybody thinks they are as good as Stella McCartney or Dolce & Gabbana, but is the untrained amateur designer as good as an MA graduate with years of experience in

industry? Of course not. What kind of design cacophony are we going to experience when everyone designs their own clothes, cars and houses?

Will consumers be able to manufacture their own designs by themselves?
The DIY design movement will go one step further when rapid prototyping enables consumers to manufacture their own goods. Materials currently in use tend to be powders bonded by adhesive, resins, liquid plastics and metals, which limit product look and product type. Once a broader range of materials can be used in rapid prototyping, it will catch on quickly, and I think that the rapid prototyping of toys and simple plastic objects will become standard in the near future.

TOP
Shah has identified a new frugality among today's consumers, which he considers to be a long-term, lasting shift. The wartime slogan 'Make Do and Mend' describes how consumers are more likely to try to make goods last longer, while the drive towards DIY design is inspiring people to make more things themselves.

CENTRE AND BOTTOM
Shah predicts that, in the future, consumers will not only manufacture more products themselves, but also grow more of their own food.

LI EDELKOORT

From her base in Paris, Dutch-born trend expert Li Edelkoort creates inspirational 'concepts', releases a variety of publications and provides a consultancy service to various industries. Edelkoort's company Trend Union produces biannual magazines for the design industries on colour trends, materials and lifestyle shifts. As president of Edelkoort Inc., a consultancy with offices in New York and Tokyo, she has a reach that extends from North America to Asia, and wields influence over some of the world's leading manufacturers. Edelkoort predicted the increasing impact of the colour white, and advised Estée Lauder to develop skincare products based on milk, which, reportedly, dramatically increased their profits. Her work also persuaded car manufacturer Nissan to offer its customers five characteristically bright colour options, which directly contributed to the success of its new line.

According to Edelkoort, trend research is not based on statistics or research, or on a drive to discover anything new. Rather, Edelkoort says that her work relies on her intuitive approach to observing behaviour and moods, and her ability to interpret them.

Post Fossil:
An Archaic Home
for the Future

Time has come for extreme change.

In the aftermath of the worst financial crisis in decades, a period of glamorous and streamlined design for design's sake has come to an end. A new generation of designers will retrace their roots, refine their earth and research their history, sometimes going back to the beginning of time.

In this process, they will form and formulate their designs around exactly these natural and sustainable materials, favouring timber, hide, pulp, fibre, blown glass, earth and fire; like contemporary

OPPOSITE
This teapot by Dutch designer Wieki Somers resembles an animal skull. It brings to mind early man's use of bones as tools and utensils, or ritual artefacts used by primitive cultures.

BELOW
Joris Laarman, a Dutch designer, makes his Bone furniture using software that replicates the growth processes of such natural objects as trees and bones. To date, Laarman has applied this biotechnology only to product design, but he also sees the potential to use it to create large-scale structures and architecture.

In the course of considering future trends within design, Edelkoort has identified a growing need for authenticity, a renewed appreciation of fundamental properties and a rediscovery of 'primitive' forms. She describes these shifts as the 'Post Fossil' trend, and claims that it can already be seen in design and architecture today. Edelkoort's identification of this trend was the basis for her touring exhibition *Post Fossil: Excavating 21st Century Creation* and a series of trend concepts that related the movement's relevance to industry. When asked to share her vision of design's future for the purposes of this book, Edelkoort responded by providing a text that she had recently written on the Post Fossil phenomenon. The text suggests that future aesthetics may unfold in a direction few experts could have anticipated.

TOP
Dutch artist Jan Eric Visser challenges conventional notions of design and architecture by turning household refuse into works of art. Visser's *Aquadyne* sculpture, made out of recycled plastics normally used for drainage and roofing, is part of his Form Follows Garbage project.

BOTTOM
The Fat Knit Hammock by Berlin-based design studio Bless updates a rudimentary item of furniture for the twenty-first-century home. Knitted from soft materials, the hammock brings an element of traditional craftsmanship to the contemporary interior.

OPPOSITE, TOP
These ceramics by Dutch designer Maaike Roozenburg are inspired by the robust ancient vessels that once characterized the primitive kitchen: bowl, jug and cooking pot.

OPPOSITE, BOTTOM
To make his Liquid Pillows chair, Dutch designer Pepe Heykoop melts foam over a metal chair frame and then coats the foam in rubber. Heykoop's 'dissolving' chair heralds a new breed of designs intended to challenge conventional ideas of structure and mass.

cavemen, they will reinvent shelter, redesign tools and man-made machines, and conceptualize archaic rituals for a more modest, contented and contained lifestyle. Like a Fred Flintstone of tomorrow.

Organic structures will be coiled and built up in dome-like mounds located in rugged settings. Earth-based clays will be developed in smooth and sophisticated ways to redefine them as the new concrete in building, accompanying the earth architecture in a rough-and-ready journey towards a more archaic contemporary existence.

Materials will be matt and humble; however, the Earth and its hidden riches also invite this generation to employ minerals, alloys and crystals, adding lustre and sometimes even sheen to their fossil-like concepts and constructions. At times, these designs will echo the essence of the *arte povera* movement, which is bound to make a revival – soon.

In touch with what can be seen as man's more animalistic side, designers will create brute and raw homes that resemble totemic termite mounds, complex honeycomb constructions and spider-web lace, possibly even incorporating animals into the making process in a new school of entomology to inspire design systems for the future.

DESIGN DIRECTORY

A

Troy Abbott
troyabbott.com

Ron Arad Associates
62 Chalk Farm Road
London NW1 8AN
United Kingdom
ronarad.co.uk

Arup
13 Fitzroy Street
London W1T 4BQ
United Kingdom
arup.com

Atracsys
Avenue du 24 Janvier 11
1020 Renens
Switzerland
atracsys.com

B

Daniele Bedini
IS in and out space
Via della Masse, 24
50056 Montelupo
Fiorentino
Florence
Italy
isspace.com

Mathias Bengtsson
Bengtsson Design
40/41 Great Castle Street
London W1W 8LU
United Kingdom
bengtssondesign.com

**David Benjamin and
Soo-in Yang**
The Living New York
thelivingnewyork.com

Bless
Eine GmbH
Ernst-Reuter Siedlung 15
13355 Berlin
Germany
bless-service.de

**Riccardo Blumer
Architect**
Via Scalette 1/b
21020 Casciago (Va)
Italy
riccardoblumer.it

Sam Buxton
sambuxton.com

C

**Vincent Callebaut
Architectures**
119, rue Manin
(Bâtiment D)
75019 Paris
France
vincent.callebaut.org

Maarten De Ceulaer
Vanderschrickstraat 59
1060 Brussels
Belgium
maartendeceulaer.com

**Kyu Che
Symbionic Design Studio**
38 Lusk Street No. 5
San Francisco, CA 94107
United States
kyuche.com

Luigi Colani
colani.de

D

Enrico Dini
d-shape.com

Winka Dubbeldam
Archi-Tectonics
11 Hubert Street
New York, NY 10013
United States
archi-tectonics.com

Dunne & Raby
13 Voss Street
London E2 6JE
United Kingdom
dunneandraby.co.uk

E

Li Edelkoort
30, boulevard Saint
  Jacques
75014 Paris
France
trendunion.com

Studio Olafur Eliasson
Christinenstrasse 18/19
Haus 2
10119 Berlin
Germany
olafureliasson.net

F

Faltazi
faltazi.com

Farsen | Schöllhammer
Ebelingstrasse 12
10249 Berlin
Germany
farsen-schoellhammer.de

David Fisher
dynamicarchitecture.net

Freedom Of Creation
Cruquiuskade 85–87
1018 AM Amsterdam
The Netherlands
freedomofcreation.com

Marco Fumagalli
Marc Arch Studio
marcarch.it

Future-Shape
Altlaufstrasse 34
85635 Höhenkirchen-
  Siegertsbrunn
Germany
future-shape.com

G

**Simone Giostra &
Partners**
55 Washington Street,
  Suite 454
Brooklyn, NY 11201
United States
sgp-architects.com

Graft
2404 Wilshire Boulevard,
  Suite 11E
Los Angeles, CA 90057
United States
graftlab.com

**Gramazio & Kohler
Architecture and Digital
Fabrication**
ETH Zurich
Building HIL, Floor F,
  Room 56
Wolfgang-Pauli-Strasse 15
8093 Zurich
Switzerland
dfab.arch.ethz.ch

Johanna Grawunder
grawunder.com

Erik Griffioen
erikgriffioen.nl

Serhan Gurkan
serhangurkan.com

H

**Noa Haim
Collective Paper
Aesthetics**
NW Binnenweg 194-B 3r
3021 GK Rotterdam
The Netherlands
collectivepaperaesthetics.
  wordpress.com

Jane Harris
Digital Design Imaging
Kingston University
River House
53–57 High Street
Kingston upon Thames
Surrey KT1 1LQ
United Kingdom
kingston.ac.uk

Simon Hasan
simonhasan.com

Jaime Hayón
Muntaner 88
08011 Barcelona
Spain
hayonstudio.com

Simon Heijdens
simonheijdens.com

Pepe Heykoop
Waalsteeg 15
1011 ER Amsterdam
The Netherlands
pepeheykoop.nl

I

**Interactive Institute
C-Studio**
Kungsgatan 54
602 33 Norrköping
Sweden
tii.se
visualiseringscenter.se

Toyo Ito & Associates, Architects
Fujiya Building
1-19-4 Shibuya
Shibuya-ku
Tokyo 150-0002
Japan
toyo-ito.co.jp

K

Astrid Krogh
Sturlasgade 14 D
2300 Copenhagen
Denmark
astridkrogh.com

Onkar Kular
52 York Hill
London SE27 0AD
United Kingdom
onkarkular.com

L

Joris Laarman Lab
Ottho Heldringstraat 3
1066 AZ Amsterdam
The Netherlands
jorislaarman.com

Max Lamb
5 Fountayne Road
Unit 11
London N15 4QL
United Kingdom
maxlamb.org

Suzanne Lee
biocouture.co.uk

Mathieu Lehanneur
14, rue des Jeuneurs
75002 Paris
France
mathieulehanneur.com

Arik Levy
29, rue des Panoyaux
75020 Paris
France
ariklevy.fr

Loop.pH
8 Springfield House
5 Tyssen Street
London E8 2LY
United Kingdom
loop.ph

Ross Lovegrove
21 Powis Mews
London W11 1JN
United Kingdom
rosslovegrove.com

M

William McDonough
700 East Jefferson Street
Charlottesville, VA 22902
United States
mcdonough.com

**Maggie Orth's/
International Fashion
Machines**
1439 East Ward Street,
   Suite B
Seattle, WA 98112
United States
ifmachines.com

J. Mayer H.
Bleibtreustrasse 54
10623 Berlin
Germany
jmayerh.de

Julian Mayor
106 Sclater Street
London E1 6HR
United Kingdom
julianmayor.com

Valentin Mellström
mellstroms.com

Molo Design
1470 Venables Street
Vancouver, BC
Canada V5L 2G7
molodesign.com

P

Philips Design
Emmasingel 24
Building HWD
5611 AZ Eindhoven
The Netherlands
design.philips.com

Bertjan Pot
Schie 34
3111 PN Schiedam
The Netherlands
bertjanpot.nl

PowerKiss
powerkiss.com

R

R&Sie(n) Architects
new-territories.com

Karim Rashid
357 West 17th Street
New York, NY 10011
United States
karimrashid.com

**Rasmus Fenhann
Furniture**
Nyrnberggade 23
2300 Copenhagen S
Denmark
fenhann.com

Realities:United
Falckensteinstrasse 47–48
10997 Berlin
Germany
realities-united.de

**Studio Maaike
Roozenburg**
Zuideinde 74–98
1541 CG Koog a/d Zaan
The Netherlands
maaikeroozenburg.nl

S

seeper
29 Waterson Street
London E2 8HT
United Kingdom
seeper.com

David Shah
Metropolitan Publishing
Saxen Weimarlaan 6
1075 CA Amsterdam
The Netherlands
view-publications.com

Hiroyuki Shinoda
Department of Information
   Physics and Computing
The University of Tokyo
7-3-1 Hongo
Bunkyo-ku
Tokyo 113-8656
Japan
alab.t.u-tokyo.ac.jp

Studio Wieki Somers
Nieuwe Haven 91
3116 AB Schiedam
The Netherlands
wiekisomers.com

Philippe Starck
36, rue Scheffer
75116 Paris
France
starck.com

Helen Storey
helenstoreyfoundation.org

Studio Wikitecture
studiowikitecture.com

Super Cilia Skin
Mitchell Joachim,
Associate Professor,
New York University
archinode.org

Hayes Raffle, Principal
Scientist, Nokia Research
Center, Palo Alto
hayesraffle.com

James Tichenor,
Creative Director,
Rockwell Group LAB
lab.rockwellgroup.com

T

Table Talk
Marcus Ericsson, John
Eriksson, Minna Gedin
and David Sjunnesson
davidsjunnesson.com

Susumu Tachi
tachilab.org

Tactility Factory
Unit 4C, Linfield Industrial
   Estate
Belfast BT12 5LA
United Kingdom
tactilityfactory.com

Makoto Tanijiri
Suppose Design Office
13-2-3F Kako-machi
Naka-ku
Hiroshima 730-0812
Japan
suppose.jp

Mette Ramsgard Thomsen
Centre for Information
   Technology and
   Architecture
School of Architecture
Royal Danish Academy of
   Fine Arts
Philip de Langes Allé 10
1435 Copenhagen
Denmark
cita.karch.dk

Jenny Tillotson
The Innovation Centre
School of Fashion and
   Textiles
Central Saint Martins
   College of Art
   and Design
Southampton Row
London WC1B 4AP
United Kingdom
smartsecondskin.com

Anne Toomey
School of Fashion
   and Textiles
Royal College of Art
Kensington Gore
London SW7 2EU
United Kingdom
rca.ac.uk

Noam Toran
noamtoran.com

V

Veech Media Architecture
Rudolfsplatz 6/2
1010 Vienna
Austria
veech-vma.com

Jan Eric Visser
janericvisser.nl

W

Moritz Waldemeyer
waldemeyer.com

Marcel Wanders Studio
PO Box 11332
1001 GH Amsterdam
The Netherlands
marcelwanders.nl

WertelOberfell Platform
15 Nassington Road
London NW3 2TX
United Kingdom
platform-net.com

Y

Ken Yeang
T.R. Hamzah & Yeang
8, Jalan 1
Taman Sri Ukay
Off Jalan Ulu Kelang
68000 Ampang
Selangor D.E.
Malaysia
trhamzahyeang.com

Tokujin Yoshioka
9-1 Daikanyama-cho
Shibuya-ku
Tokyo 150-0034
Japan
tokujin.com

BIBLIOGRAPHY

BOOKS AND JOURNAL ARTICLES

Paola Antonelli and Hugh Aldersey-Williams, *Design and the Elastic Mind*, New York (The Museum of Modern Art) 2008

Federico Barbagli *et al.*, eds, *Multi-point Interaction with Real and Virtual Objects*, Vienna (Springer) 2005

Alexander Bard and Jan Söderqvist, *Netocracy: The New Power Elite and Life After Capitalism*, London (Reuters) 2002

Jannice Benyus, *Biomimicry: Innovation Inspired by Nature*, New York (Harper Perennial) 2002

James Canton, *The Extreme Future: The Top Trends That Will Reshape the World in the Next 20 Years*, New York (Plume Books) 2007

——, *Technofutures: How Leading-Edge Technologies Will Transform Business in the 21st Century*, Carlsbad, Calif. (Hay House) 1999

Craig DeLancey, *Passionate Engines: What Emotions Reveal About Mind and Artificial Intelligence*, Oxford (Oxford University Press) 2004

Rasshied Din, *New Retail*, London (Conran Octopus) 2000

Winka Dubbeldam, *AT-INdex*, New York (Princeton Architectural Press) 2006

James Gibson, *The Senses Considered as Perceptual Systems*, Westport, Conn. (Greenwood Press) 1983

Ingrid Giertz-Mårtenson, *Att se in i framtiden. En studie av trendanalys inom modebranschen* (Looking into the Future: An Analysis of Fashion Forecasting), Stockholm (Department of Ethnology, Stockholm University) 2006

David Gissen, *Big and Green: Towards Sustainable Architecture in the 21st Century*, New York (Princeton Architectural Press) 2009

——, *Subnature: Architecture's Other Environments*, New York (Princeton Architectural Press) 2003

David Goldberg and Kumara Sastry, *Genetic Algorithms: The Design of Innovation*, Vienna (Springer) 2010

Martin Grunwald, ed., *Human Haptic Perception: Basics and Applications*, Basel (Birkhäuser) 2008

Thorsten Klooster, *Smart Surfaces and Their Application in Architecture and Design*, Basel (Birkhäuser) 2009

Suzanne Lee, *Fashioning the Future: Tomorrow's Wardrobe*, London (Thames & Hudson) 2007

Bjørn Lomborg, *The Skeptical Environmentalist: Measuring the Real State of the World*, Cambridge (Cambridge University Press) 2001

William McDonough and Michael Braungart, *Cradle to Cradle: Remaking the Way We Make Things*, Portland, Ore. (North Point Press) 2002

Maria Mackinney-Valentin, *On the Nature of Trends: A Study of Trend Mechanisms in Contemporary Fashion*, PhD dissertation, The Danish Design School, Copenhagen, 2010

Matilda McQuaid, ed., *Extreme Textiles: Designing for High Performance*, New York (Princeton Architectural Press) 2005

Gary Marx, *Sixteen Trends: Their Profound Impact on Our Future*, Alexandria, Va. (Educational Research Service) 2006

William J. Mitchell, *City of Bits*, Boston (MIT Press) 1996

——, *E-topia: Urban Life, Jim – But Not as We Know It*, Boston (MIT Press) 2000

Toshiko Mori, ed., *Immaterial/Ultramaterial*, New York (George Braziller) 2002

Jennifer Owings Dewey, *Animal Architecture*, London (Orchard Books) 1991

Bradley Quinn, *The Fashion of Architecture*, Oxford (Berg) 2003

——, *Techno Fashion*, Oxford (Berg) 2002

——, *Textile Futures*, Oxford (Berg) 2010

——, ed., *UltraMaterials*, London (Thames & Hudson) 2007

Karim Rashid, *Design Your Life: Rethinking the Way You Live, Work, Love and Play*, New York (HarperCollins) 2006

——, *I Want to Change the World*, New York (Rizzoli) 2001

——, *KarimSpace*, New York (Rizzoli) 2009

Martin Raymond, *The Trend Forecaster's Handbook*, London (Laurence King) 2010

Gabriel Robles-De-La-Torre, 'The Importance of the Sense of Touch in Virtual and Real Environments', *IEEE Multimedia* 13, 2006, pp. 24–30

Kevin Sahr *et al.*, 'Geodesic Discrete Global Grid Systems', *Cartography and Geographic Information Science* 30, 2003, pp. 121–34

Ruth Slavid, *Extreme Architecture: Building for Challenging Environments*, London (Laurence King) 2009

Michael Speaks, ed., *Winka Dubbeldam, Architect*, Rotterdam (010 Publishers) 1996

Lars Spuybroek, *NOX: Machining Architecture*, London (Thames & Hudson) 2004

Carolyn Steel, *Hungry City: How Food Shapes Our Lives*, London (Vintage) 2009

Henrik Vejlgaard, *Anatomy of a Trend*, New York (McGraw-Hill) 2008

Peter Zellner, *Hybrid Space: New Digital Forms in Architecture*, London (Thames & Hudson) 2000

WEBSITES AND ONLINE PUBLICATIONS

Copenhagen Institute for Future Studies
cifs.dk

Futuribles
futuribles.com

Kairos Future
kairosfuture.com

Ocean Energy Council
oceanenergycouncil.com

Seed Magazine
seedmagazine.com

Trend Union
trendunion.com

Trendethnography
trendethnography.com

United Minds
unitedminds.se

View Network
view-network.com

View Publications
view-publications.com

WGSN
wgsn.com

World Future Society
wfs.org

ACKNOWLEDGEMENTS

This book would not have been possible without the
support of the designers and researchers featured between
its covers. I thank each of them for giving generously
of their time to provide images of and information about
their work. I would also like to thank everyone at Merrell
Publishers for their commitment to the project, and for
making this book such a pleasure to write.

Design Futures is dedicated to Markus Sterky, a friend who
has always inspired me with his cutting-edge approach,
and who introduced me to new technologies and fresh
ways of seeing the world around me.

PICTURE CREDITS

l = left; r = right; t = top; b = bottom; c = centre

© Acoustical Surfaces Inc.: 94b; Advanced Civil Engineering Materials Research Laboratory (ACE-MRL) at the University of Michigan: 109t; © Archimation: 31bl, 31br; © 2009 Archi-Tectonics: 17t, 17b, 69 (all); Architecture and Digital Fabrication/DFAB: 63b; Arkema: 93bl; Atracsys: 186, 186–87, 187, 189; Bengtsson Design: 161t; Bengtsson Design/Jeppe Gudmundsen-Holmgreen: 161b; Bengtsson Design/Maurizio Camagna: 123 (all); Biosphère, Environment Canada: 25t, 25b; Bless: 228b; Stéphane Briolant: 153t, 153b; Matteo Brogi: 66t, 66b, 67; Canon: 171, 190–91; Kyu Che: 22t, 22b; Concrete Canvas Ltd/Phillip Greer: 93t, 98t, 98b, 99t, 99b; Courtesy Danish Fashion Institute: 113; Courtesy DSM Dyneema: 83t, 83b; Dunne & Raby/Per Tingleff: 139t, 139b; © DuPont, reproduced with permission: 115b, 219, 220; echelman.com. © João Ferrand: 79b; Electrolux Design Lab: 58t, 58b; Olaf Eliasson: 149t, 149b; Faltazi: 59; Farsen | Schöllhammer: 150; Rasmus Fenhann: 151b; FOC: 2, 129t, 129b, 144–45, 146br, 147, 194; Marco Fumagalli (photography and design)/Electrolux (induction cooking system)/3B (doors)/Sadun (post-formed top): 60t, 60b, 61; Courtesy Galerie Magnus Müller, Berlin. Photography: © Christina Dimitriadis. Reproduced with permission of J. Mayer H. Architects: 105t; Claude Germain: 163c; © GKD/ag4: 79c, 85b, 216–17; © Mathias Gmachl/Loop.pH: 8–9; GRL – Laboratoire Arkema: 79tr; © 2000–01 Sabine Gruber, reprinted with permission of Veech Media

Architecture: 93br; Peter Guenzel: 128bl, 128br; Okan Guler/Serhan Gurkan: 151tl, 151tr; Noa Haim: 97; Hanse Haus GmbH: 57 (all); Jane Harris/Mike Dawson (3D CG)/Shelley Fox (fashion design): 193c; Jane Harris/Mike Dawson (3D CG)/Elli Garnett (performer/choreography): 179t, 179b; Jane Harris/Mike Dawson (3D CG)/Ruth Gibson (performer/choreography): 193t, 193b; Simon Hasan: 156t, 156b, 157t, 157b; Simon Heijdens: 143 (all), 154; Courtesy Hermès Japon: 165t; Guy Hills (photography)/Wendy Latham (illustration): 49 (all); Maarten van Houten: 229tl, 229tr; © Veronique Huyghe: 136 (all), 137t, 137b, 163t, 163b; Ingeo/Fashion Helmet: 115t; Inovenso: 103br; iRobot Corporation: 64 (all); Jean Godecharle Fotografie: 52; Courtesy Karim Rashid Inc.: 37, 38; © Fabien Thouvenin Klane: 132; © Lisa Klappe (photography)/Alissia Melka-Teichroew (design)/FOC (production): 146t, 195t, 195b; Nienke Klunder: 40t, 40b, 41; Onkar Kular: 142; Kengo Kuma: 44 (all); Kuramochi + Oguma: 33 (all); Joris Laarman: 226; Niki Lackner/Kunsthaus Graz, Peter Cook and Colin Fournier: 206 (all); Suzanne Lee: 115c, 116, 121tl, 121tr, 121b; Suzanne Lee/Santiago Arribas Peña/Science Museum, London: 121cl, 121cr; LG Hausys: 90–91; © Loop.pH Ltd, reproduced with permission: 88b; Aoife Ludlow: 119tl; Alex Maguire: 76–77, 107, 119bl, 119br; Peter Mallet: 140–41; Maurer United Architects: 202–203; mellstroms.com: 223; C. Meyer: 71b; © 2010 Milliken & Company: 85tl; Courtesy Minelco Ltd: 79tl; © Bip Mistry: 43b; Molo: 199; Alastair Mucklow: 119tr; Mike Nicolaassen:

146bl; Kurt Nielsen: 212–13; Nous Gallery: 152; Courtesy ossur.com: 81; Margaret Pate. © CSIRO: 105bl; © 2010 Peratech Ltd: 103tl, 103tr; © Philips Design, reproduced with permission: 85tr, 87, 211; Yael Pincus: 172–73; © Marie-Françoise Plissart: 14tl, 14tr; Marie-Françoise Plissart (photography)/Philippe Samyn and Partners (architects): 19t, 20–21; © Bertjan Pot, reproduced with permission: 159; © PowerKiss: 181bl, 181br; Pramac S.p.A.: 209; R&Sie(n): 19b, 27, 65t, 65b, 200t, 200b, 205 (all); © 2004 Hayes Raffle: 110t, 110b; © Felipe Ribon: 54–55 (all); Gaetan Robillard: 130–31; © Philippe Samyn and Partners, Studio Valle Progettazioni, Buro Happold Ltd: 13; Dirk Schaper: 45t, 45b; © SDL: 31tr, 31c; Seeper: 181t; Seeper/Toyota: 176–77; Sensitile Systems: 88t; Serving Media: 228t; David Shah: 225 (all); Shinoda Lab, University of Tokyo: 175; © Studio AMD: 14b, 31tl; Studio Pepe Heykoop: 229b; Studio Wieki Somers: 227; TableTalk: 182 (all); © Tactility Factory: 94t; © Mette Ramsgard Thomsen, reproduced with permission: 43t; Tokujin Yoshioka Inc.: 127, 160 (all), 165b; Noam Toran/Frank Thurston: 134l, 134r, 135; Leo Torri: 46, 47, 71t; Courtesy Toshiba: 50, 51t, 51b; © Moritz Waldemeyer: endpapers, 75t, 75b, 105br, 167t, 167b, 185; Francis Ware: 128t; Simon Wood/Turf Design Studio: 28, 29 (all); WowWee Robotics: 63t.

The publisher has made every effort to trace and contact copyright holders of the material reproduced in this book. It will be happy to correct in subsequent editions any errors or omissions that are brought to its attention.

INDEX